500

cupcakes

500
cupcakes

NEW EDITION! the only cupcake compendium you'll ever need

Fergal Connolly & Judith Fertig

SELLERS
PUBLISHING

A Quintet Book

Published by Sellers Publishing, Inc.
161 John Roberts Road, South Portland, Maine 04106
Visit our Web site: www.sellerspublishing.com
E-mail: rsp@rsvp.com

This edition published in 2012

ISBN: 978-1-4162-0631-6
e-ISBN: 978-1-4162-0675-0
Library of Congress Control Number: 2010933890
QTT.LCU2

This book was conceived, designed, and produced by
Quintet Publishing Limited
4th Floor, Sheridan House
114-116 Western Road
Hove BN3 1DD
United Kingdom

ORIGINAL EDITION:
Project Editor: Jenny Doubt
Associate Project Editor: Rebecca Warren
Editor: Marianne Canty
Art Director: Roland Codd
Photographer: Ian Garlick
Home Economist: Fergal Connolly
Publisher: Judith More
Creative Director: Richard Dewing
Managing Editor: Jane Laing

UPDATED EDITION:
Food Stylist: Lorna Brash
Photographer: Ian Garlick
Art Director: Michael Charles
Editorial Assistants: Carly Beckerman-Boys, Holly Willsher
Managing Editor: Donna Gregory
Publisher: Mark Searle

10 9 8 7 6 5

Printed in China by 1010 Printing International Ltd.

contents

introduction

Whether it's their individual size, their pretty frosting, or just their ability to bring back fond memories of childhood, cupcakes really do have ultimate treat-appeal. Every generation seems to love them, and even the most curmudgeonly among us will find it hard to fight off a smile when presented with a plateful of cupcakes.

Cupcakes come in many shapes and guises, but the one thing they all have in common is that they're small, individual-sized cakes baked in a muffin pan or cup-shaped molds, which are often lined with pleated foil or paper baking cups. You can make cupcakes by baking almost any cake batter in a cup-shaped mold. Classic yellow cake or pound cake mixtures are particularly popular, but gingerbread, carrot cakes, fruit cakes, yeasted cakes, and brownies can all be transformed into cupcakes. They can be frosted, decorated, glazed, dusted, or left unadorned — and whichever you choose, they're sure to be delicious.

As well as making traditional baked cupcakes, you can steam some mixtures to make dense, moist desserts, like bread pudding. You can make other cupcakes using the no-bake method, in which you spoon a mixture of melted and dry ingredients into cupcake molds and chill or leave them to set. These unbaked cupcakes are usually served unfrosted, or simply dusted with a little confectioners' sugar or unsweetened cocoa powder.

types of cupcakes

Cupcakes go by many different names. Some describe specific types of cakes, while others are more generic, but whatever name they go by, cupcakes can be found worldwide. Even in Southeast Asia you'll find little cupcakes. In the Philippines, mooncakes — rice cakes steamed in banana leaf cups — are a delicious treat.

Many great classic cupcakes can be served frosted — chocolate buttercream cupcakes (page 32) are served with a generous smear of rich chocolate frosting. Others, such as vanilla cupcakes (page 21) are delicious without frosting. Madeleines are classic French cupcakes that are also served plain. Baked in a shell-shaped mold, they are traditionally made with a mixture of egg yolks beaten with sugar and lemon zest, then combined with flour, hazelnut butter, and whisked egg whites. You will find a modern recipe for madeleines on page 39.

Queen cakes are a traditional British cupcake made with a creamed butter mixture combination not unlike the vanilla cupcake mixture, with currants, and lemon zest added. Traditionally, Queen cakes were baked in small, fluted molds, but today they are usually baked in paper-lined or greased muffin pans.

frosting cupcakes

Although some cupcakes are served plain, it is the frosting that makes many cupcakes. Whether it's a thick smear of cream cheese frosting or an intricately decorated cake topped with fondant decorations, it's the topping that often causes the greatest delight, not just for the sweet, luscious flavor it adds to a simple cake. Once frosted, cupcakes are best eaten right away, and if you intend to store or freeze them, don't frost them first. Whether you are a child or adult, beginner or advanced baker, once you get started on the recipes in this book, you'll realize just how fun baking and decorating cupcakes can be!

basic equipment

Most cupcakes are incredibly simple to make, and you'll only need a few pieces
of equipment.

scales, measuring cups & spoons
Accurate weighing scales and/or calibrated measuring cups, as well as proper measuring
spoons, are essential for successful baking. If the proportions of ingredients are incorrect, the
cupcake may not rise and/or set properly.

mixing bowls and spoons
You will need a medium-sized bowl and wooden spoon for mixing most cupcake batters.
Smaller-sized bowls are useful for mixing small quantities. A large metal spoon is useful for
folding ingredients into delicate whisked mixtures. Unless otherwise stipulated, use a
medium-sized bowl for the recipes in this book.

sieves
You will need a large sieve for sifting dry ingredients such as flour and a small one for
dusting icing sugar or cocoa over baked cupcakes.

baking cups
Pleated paper or foil baking cups are available in many sizes, from tiny petit four cups for
making mini cupcakes, to giant baking cups for extra-large treats.

muffin pans

Muffin pans are the most user-friendly pans for making standard cupcakes. The standard muffin pan has 6 or 12 cup-shaped indentations. You can line them with paper baking cups, or simply grease them before filling them with batter. The standard muffin cup is approximately 2 1/2 in. (6 cm.) in diameter. Mini and jumbo muffin pans are a great way to vary shapes and sizes of your cupcakes. Mini muffin pans have 12 or 24 cup-shaped indentations and are 2 in. (5 cm.) in diameter, whereas jumbo muffin pans have 6 cup-shaped indentations, with each cup measuring 4 in. (10 cm.) in diameter.

other cupcake molds

You can bake cupcakes in other molded pans. Shell-shaped madeleine pans are widely available. You may also find other pans with decorative, ridged cups in a variety of sizes. Individual stainless steel molds or ceramic cups can also be used to bake cupcakes.

timers

Perfect timing is essential for success, so always use a timer when baking. Accurate digital timers are inexpensive and well worth the investment.

wire racks

Leave most cupcakes in the pan to cool for 5 minutes before transferring them to a wire rack to cool completely. Wire racks come in a variety of shapes and sizes.

other equipment

Electric mixers can save time and are great for combining all-in-one cake mixtures. The mixer should be set on medium speed unless otherwise indicated. A sharp, serrated knife with a pointed end can help slice the tops off cupcakes or make a hollow in which to spoon filling.

basic ingredients

Most cupcake mixtures have four basic ingredients: fat, sugar, eggs, and flour. Other ingredients, such as chocolate, nuts, and dried fruit, are frequently added.

eggs
Eggs enrich cupcake mixtures and help to bind ingredients together. For the best results, use eggs at room temperature. When whisking egg whites, be sure to use a clean, grease-free bowl. Eggs should always be lightly beaten before adding to the recipe unless otherwise stated.

butter & other fats
Sweet (unsalted) butter is usually best for cupcake mixtures; it gives a wonderfully rich flavor. For creamed cupcake mixtures, use butter at room temperature; for cut-in mixtures, use cold, firm butter; and for melted mixtures, dice the butter before gently warming it. Margarine, white cooking fats, and mild-tasting vegetable oils sometimes replace butter and are a good choice for those with a dairy intolerance or allergy. Butter and cream cheese should always be softened before adding to the recipe unless otherwise stated.

flour & flour alternatives
Most cupcake mixtures call for self-rising flour or all-purpose flour, with the addition of a leavening agent. Whole wheat flour is sometimes used, but it produces cupcakes with a heavier, denser texture. Non-wheat flours, often combined with wheat flour, may also be used. These include cornmeal, oatmeal, cornstarch, and rice flour. Ground nuts may be used in place of flour and are particularly good for gluten-free cupcakes.

sugar & other sweeteners

There are many different types of sugar, all of which add their own unique taste and texture to cupcake mixtures. Refined white sugars add sweetness, while brown sugars add flavor and color as well. Brown sugar should always be packed when being measured. The texture of the sugar will also affect the cupcake. Granulated sugar is most frequently used for cupcakes, but raw sugar, and moist sugars such as brown sugar, are also used. For a finer texture, substitute granulated sugar for superfine, or make your own by pulsing granulated sugar in a food processor until very fine. Confectioners' sugar is generally used for dusting cupcakes and making frosting. Light corn syrup, maple syrup, honey, and molasses can also be used in cupcakes, either in place of, or alongside, sugar. They give a distinctive taste and texture, and are a frequent addition to melted cake mixtures.

other ingredients & flavorings

Dried fruits, nuts, and seeds are a popular addition to cupcake mixtures. Dried fruits add natural sweetness, so you may be able to use less sugar than in a plain cupcake mixture. Different dried fruits are often interchangeable in recipes.

Fresh fruit such as mashed bananas, apples, pineapples, and berries may also be folded into cupcake batters. Frozen fruit may be substituted for fresh in the recipes in this book. Thoroughly thaw and drain before adding to the recipe. Chocolate may be used to flavor or bind cake mixtures or to decorate baked cupcakes. For the recipes in this book, you'll need unsweetened cocoa powder, chocolate chips or chunks, and different varieties of baking chocolate in your pantry. Vanilla-flavored pudding or pie filling may be substituted for custard. Always assume that herbs used in the recipes are dried, unless fresh is specified. Other ingredients and flavorings include marshmallows, spices, cheese, vanilla, coffee, citrus zest, almond extract, orange flower water and rosewater, and liqueurs.

making cupcakes

There are four main types of cupcake mixtures. The order in which ingredients are added and the way they are combined — for example, beaten or folded in — will affect the final texture of the cupcakes.

preparing the pan
When the recipe calls for the pan to be greased, you may use any fat you choose. Smear a little butter, margarine, or olive oil on a paper towel and wipe each cup thoroughly. Low-calorie sprays can also be used for this purpose. Fill any empty cups in the pan with water.

creamed mixtures
For creamed mixtures, you begin by creaming the sugar and fat together to make a light, fluffy mixture before beating in eggs. Self-rising flour (or all-purpose flour and a leavening agent such as baking powder) is then folded in, along with any other flavoring ingredients.

The mixture should then be poured into baking cups and baked immediately. Moisture and heat cause tiny bubbles of carbon dioxide to be released, producing cupcakes with a light and fluffy texture.

Sometimes baking powder may be replaced with baking soda plus an acidic ingredient, such as vinegar, cider, or buttermilk. These substitutes all work effectively to help the cupcake rise while it is baking.

all-in-one mixtures
This technique is literally "all in one": Put all the ingredients in a bowl and beat them until smooth. Then fold in additional ingredients such as dried fruit and pour the batter into the pan(s) for baking.

whisked mixtures
The classic cupcake mixture is whisked. Begin by whisking eggs and sugar. Then fold in the flour and other dry ingredients. The air bubbles expand in the heat, causing the cupcake to rise and giving it a spongy texture.

general baking tips
When adding batter to a pan, you may either spoon or pour the batter into the cups. Each cup should be two-thirds full unless otherwise stated. When baking, the pans should be placed in the center of the oven. As oven temperatures vary by model, test cupcakes for doneness a few minutes before the end of the baking time. If a skewer inserted into the center of the cupcake comes out clean, it is done. If your cupcakes are brown on top but not cooked through, try lowering your oven temperature.

storing
Cupcakes made with a high proportion of fat can be stored in an airtight container for several days. Low-fat cupcakes are usually best eaten on the day of making. For the best results, store cakes unfrosted, and frost on the day of serving. Cupcakes can also be frozen, unfrosted, in an airtight container for up to 3 months.

decorating cupcakes

Cupcakes are the treats that you can really go to town on when it comes to decoration. A simple spoonful of frosting with a cherry on top or a drizzle of melted chocolate is just the start. Supermarkets and specialty cooking stores sell a host of ingredients and equipment to help you — from food coloring and ready-made frostings to edible sugared flowers and brightly colored candy. Here are a few ideas that will help you transform the simplest cupcakes into a stunning dessert.

getting started
If you're going for simply frosted cupcakes — perhaps with a dollop of frosting and a big colored candy or whole nut on top — leave the cupcake as it is, with its domed top. However, if you want to go for a more intricately decorated cupcake — perhaps with a patterned frosting on top, or lots of candies — slice off the top of the cake to give you a flat surface. Always wait for cupcakes to cool before frosting them.

decorating cupcakes before baking
Unbaked cupcakes can be sprinkled with coarse sugar; whole, chopped, or flaked nuts or dried fruit; or a piece of fresh fruit such as a slice of apple or peach. Don't top them with anything too heavy or it may sink into the batter during baking.

fondant frosting
Perfect for rolling out and draping over cupcakes, this firm frosting can also be colored and made into shapes to decorate cakes. You can make it yourself, but it's much easier to buy ready-to-roll fondant frosting and color it yourself. Simply add a few drops of food coloring and then thoroughly knead the fondant. Repeat until the desired color is achieved.

colored candy & cake decorations

Candy and colored sprinkles are easy ways to decorate cupcakes. Alternately, look in specialty cooking stores for sugar flowers, pastel-colored almonds, and other edible decorations. First top the cupcakes with frosting or melted chocolate, then allow it to set slightly before pressing on the decorations. If you prefer a cupcake without too much frosting, use only a small blob to attach individual candies or decorations — they'll look just as good but won't be nearly so sweet.

fresh fruit

Summer berries look delightful (and taste delectable) on top of frosted cupcakes. They're particularly good on cakes topped with buttercream or cream cheese frosting. Or even simpler, just spoon a big dollop of heavy cream on top of each cupcake and top with a few fresh raspberries or strawberries.

simple fillings

The simplest filling is flavored heavy cream. Try sweetening heavy cream with a little confectioners' sugar and adding a few drops of vanilla or peppermint extract, rosewater, or citrus zest. Honey and maple syrup make good flavorings, as do liqueurs such as Cointreau.

moldable chocolate

Form ruffles, roses, tiny fruits and vegetables, and many other shapes with this sweet, malleable mixture. If you like, tint and flavor the chocolate after adding the corn syrup. To work with this chocolate, generously dust a flat surface, your hands, and any utensils with confectioners' sugar. To make moldable white chocolate: In a double boiler, melt 1 lb. white chocolate. Stir in 1/2 cup corn syrup until the mixture becomes smooth and glossy. Add a little more corn syrup if the chocolate is still grainy. Cover and refrigerate until ready to use. Makes 2 1/2 cups. To make moldable dark chocolate, prepare the basic recipe, substituting semisweet chocolate for white and adding 1/4 cup additional light corn syrup.

serving ideas & cupcake gifts

Cupcakes are often associated with children, but offer a plate of cupcakes to grown adults and you're sure to see their faces light up. Whether it's a rack of warm, wholesome little treats or a glittering cake stand piled high with pretty, pastel-colored confections, cupcakes are always a hit and seem to appeal to every generation.

cakes on the move
Baked in their own wrappers, these lovely cakes aren't just for eating at home. An individual, portion-sized cake is great for eating on the move — whether it's a treat to go in a lunchbox, an energy-boosting snack to take on a long walk, or an easy dessert to serve at a picnic.

dashing desserts
There's something wonderfully informal yet utterly appealing about cupcakes that makes them a great alternative to dessert after a special meal. Who's got time to make a dessert after an appetizer and main course — and who's really got room to fit one in? Why not bring out a plate of sophisticated cupcakes with coffee instead? You're sure to get just as much praise as you would for a dessert that takes hours to make.

celebrating with cupcakes
Big celebration cakes are a thing of the past. What everyone wants now is a towering pile of cupcakes. For birthdays, pile up cupcakes on a plate and stick them with birthday candles and baby indoor sparklers to really get the celebrations going. This alternative to the traditional cake is particularly good for kids' parties, where little children can struggle with a big slice of cake — or for adult parties where everyone is trying to watch their waistline!

Huge, tiered wedding cakes are off the agenda for those in the know. For a real impact at your wedding, go for pretty white wedding cupcakes piled high on a cake stand or arranged in tiers. It makes serving so much easier — and guests will love them.

special gifts

Cupcakes make great gifts, and you're sure to put a smile on the face of the recipient. They're usually best packed in a single layer, with a little tissue paper tucked around them to make sure they don't shift as you transport them. Pretty boxes with clear plastic lids are a good choice, particularly for cupcakes with decorative frosting. They're available from stationery and department stores, so look around and see what you can find. Flat baskets make another pretty way to deliver your cupcakes. Arrive at a brunch party with a basket full of cupcakes and your host — and the other guests — will love you for them!

Cupcakes with a firm frosting (such as fondant or royal frosting) can look pretty wrapped up individually in clear cellophane. Cut out a large square of cellophane, place a cupcake in the center, then pull up the edges around the cake and tie with ribbon. These individually wrapped cakes make great going-home presents after a kids' party or festive wedding favors. You can also decorate the foil or paper baking cups that contain the cupcakes. Try tying ribbon around each baking cup, or cut out a round of pretty fabric, place the cupcake in the center, and tie up firmly with coordinating ribbon.

classic cupcakes

These cupcakes have delighted generations.

From the classic combination of apple and

cinnamon to the irresistibly rich pairing of rum

and raisin, all the best-loved recipes are here.

spanish orange syrup cupcakes

see variations page 42

Make these sticky cupcakes ahead of time to let the syrup soak through.

for the cupcakes
2 medium, seedless sweet oranges,
    peeled and roughly chopped
1/2 cup (1 stick) sweet butter
1 cup granulated sugar
2 large eggs
1/2 cup semolina
1/2 cup almond meal

1/2 cup cake flour
1/2 tsp. baking powder
1/4 tsp. salt

for the syrup
1 peeled orange rind, from cupcake recipe
1/2 cup granulated sugar
1 cup water

Preheat the oven to 325°F (160°C). Place 12 paper baking cups in a muffin pan. In a saucepan, cover the oranges with 1 cup water. Simmer until tender, about 15 minutes. Cool. Drain the oranges and purée in a food processor. In a bowl, beat the butter and sugar with an electric mixer until light. Slowly beat in the eggs. Stir in the rest of the ingredients, along with the orange purée, until well combined. Spoon the mixture into the cups. Bake for 22 to 25 minutes or until a cake tester inserted in the center comes out clean. Remove pan from the oven and cool.

To make the syrup, thinly slice the orange rind, removing the pith. Cut the orange rind into thin strips. In a pan, bring the sugar and water to a simmer, stirring to dissolve the sugar. Add the orange strips and boil uncovered for 5 minutes, or until tender. With a toothpick, prick 5 holes in each cupcake and pour the warm syrup over them. Then remove the cupcakes and cool on a rack. Store in an airtight container for up to 2 days.

Makes 1 dozen

vanilla cupcakes

see variations page 43

The grand dame of cupcakes. If you can get vanilla sugar, use half regular and half vanilla sugar. This will really enhance the vanilla flavor.

1 cup (2 sticks) sweet butter, softened
1 cup granulated sugar
2 cups cake flour
2 tsp. baking powder

1 tsp. salt
4 large eggs
1/2 cup buttermilk
1 1/2 tsp. vanilla extract

Preheat the oven to 350°F (175°C). Place 18 paper baking cups in muffin pans.

Place all the ingredients in a medium bowl and beat with an electric mixer until smooth and pale, about 2 to 3 minutes.

Spoon the mixture into the cups. Bake for 20 minutes or until a cake tester inserted in the center comes out clean.

Remove the pans from the oven and cool for 5 minutes. Then remove the cupcakes and cool on a rack.

Store in an airtight container for up to 3 days, or freeze for up to 3 months.

Makes 1 1/2 dozen

gingerbread pots

see variations page 44

You could make these dense, sticky gingerbread cupcakes in terra cotta pots to give them a rustic charm. The sharp lemon drizzle helps to cut the sweetness of the gingerbread.

for the gingerbread
1 cup cake flour
1 cup white whole wheat flour
1 tbsp. baking powder
4 tsp. ground ginger
1 tsp. cinnamon
1 cup packed unrefined brown sugar
2 large eggs

1/2 cup honey
1/2 cup butter, melted
3/4 cup milk
2 tbsp. roughly chopped candied ginger

for the drizzle
1 cup confectioners' sugar
5 tbsp. lemon juice

Preheat the oven to 350°F (175°C). Place 12 paper baking cups in a muffin pan or line 12 small terra cotta pots with baking parchment. Sift the flours, baking powder, ginger, and cinnamon into a large bowl. In a medium bowl combine the remaining ingredients and beat with an electric mixer until smooth, about 2 to 3 minutes. Stir into the dry ingredients. Spoon the batter into the cups.

Bake for 20 minutes or until a cake tester inserted in the center comes out clean. Remove pan or pots from the oven and cool for 10 minutes. Then remove cupcakes and cool on a rack. To make the drizzle, sift the confectioners' sugar into a bowl and slowly add the lemon juice, stirring until just combined. Drizzle over the tops of the cupcakes. Store in an airtight container for up to 3 days.

Makes 1 dozen

lemon butterfly cupcakes

see variations page 45

You'll love these delicate little numbers, which can be served with tea or as a dessert.

for the cupcakes
1 cup (2 sticks) sweet butter, softened
1 cup granulated sugar
2 cups cake flour
2 tsp. baking powder
1 tsp. salt
4 large eggs
1/2 cup buttermilk
1 tsp. vanilla extract

for the frosting
1/2 cup (1 stick) sweet butter
2 cups confectioners' sugar, sifted
1 tsp. vanilla extract
1 tbsp. lemon zest

Preheat the oven to 350°F (175°C). Place 18 paper baking cups in muffin pans. Combine all ingredients for the cupcakes in a large bowl and beat with an electric mixer until smooth and pale, about 2 to 3 minutes. Spoon the batter into the cups.

Bake for 20 minutes. Remove pans from the oven and cool for 5 minutes. Then remove the cupcakes and cool on a rack. Prepare the frosting by beating the butter, confectioners' sugar, vanilla, and lemon zest until smooth. Cut a slice from the top of each cake and cut it into two. Pipe the frosting onto the flattened top of each cupcake. Then place the half-circles of cake at an angle on each side of the frosting.

Store unfrosted in an airtight container for up to 3 days, or freeze for up to 3 months.

Makes 1 1/2 dozen

rum & raisin cupcakes

see variations page 46

Use dark rum in this recipe to give these cupcakes a warm Caribbean feel.

for the cupcakes
1/2 cup (3 1/2 oz.) raisins
3 tbsp. dark rum
1 cup (2 sticks) sweet butter, softened
1 cup granulated sugar
2 cups cake flour
2 tsp. baking powder

1 tsp. salt
4 large eggs
1/2 cup buttermilk

for the syrup
5 tbsp. dark rum
2 tbsp. unpacked light brown sugar

Soak the raisins in the rum for 2 to 3 hours or overnight to soften them. Drain. Preheat the oven to 350°F (175°C). Place 18 paper baking cups in muffin pans. Combine all the cupcake ingredients in a large bowl and beat with an electric mixer until smooth and pale, about 2 to 3 minutes. Stir in the raisins. Spoon the batter into the cups. Bake for 20 minutes.

While the cupcakes are in the oven, combine the syrup ingredients in a pan. Over low heat, dissolve the sugar in the rum. Simmer for 5 minutes, then remove from the heat. Remove pans from the oven. With a toothpick, prick 5 holes in each cupcake and pour the warm syrup over them. Then remove the cupcakes and cool on a rack.

Store in an airtight container for up to 3 days, or freeze for up to 3 months.

Makes 1 1/2 dozen

mini raspberry &
coconut cupcakes

see variations page 47

The inspiration for these cupcakes came from the classic English Bakewell tart.

3 tbsp. ground almonds
1/2 cup (2 1/2 oz.) flaked coconut
1 1/2 cups confectioners' sugar, sifted
1 1/2 cups all-purpose flour
1 tsp. baking powder

1/2 cup (1 stick) sweet butter, melted
5 egg whites
1 cup fresh or thawed, frozen raspberries
2 tbsp. shredded coconut

Preheat the oven to 375°F (190°C). Place 24 mini ceramic baking cups on a cookie sheet.

In a large bowl, combine the ground almonds, coconut, confectioners' sugar, flour, and baking powder. Stir in the butter, followed by the egg whites.

Spoon the mixture into the cups. Drop a raspberry and some of the shredded coconut on top of each cupcake. Bake for 12 to 15 minutes or until lightly browned. Remove the cups from the oven and cool for 5 minutes. Then remove the cupcakes and cool on a rack.

Store in an airtight container for up to 2 days, or freeze in sealed containers for up to 3 months.

Makes 2 dozen

carrot & walnut cupcakes

see variations page 48

Carrot cake somehow doesn't seem to be as naughty as other cakes!

for the cupcakes
1 cup (2 sticks) sweet butter, softened
1 cup granulated sugar
2 cups cake flour
2 tsp. baking powder
1 tsp. salt
4 large eggs
1/2 cup buttermilk
1 tsp. allspice
1 cup (3 1/2 oz.) chopped walnuts

1 cup freshly shredded carrots
2 tbsp. golden raisins

for the frosting
1 cup cream cheese, softened
1 1/2 cups confectioners' sugar, sifted
1 tbsp. lemon juice
1 tsp. vanilla extract
3 tbsp. chopped walnuts

Preheat the oven to 350°F (175°C). Place 18 baking cups in muffin pans. Combine the butter, sugar, flour, baking powder, salt, eggs, and buttermilk in a large bowl and beat with an electric mixer until smooth, about 2 to 3 minutes. Stir in the rest of the ingredients. Spoon the batter into the cups. Bake for 20 minutes. Remove pans from the oven and cool for 5 minutes. Then remove the cupcakes and cool on a rack. To make the frosting, slowly beat the cream cheese and confectioners' sugar in a large bowl with an electric mixer until creamy and soft. Add the lemon juice and vanilla and beat briskly until well combined. Spread the frosting liberally onto the cooled cupcakes and garnish with the chopped walnuts.

Store unfrosted for up to 3 days in an airtight container, or freeze for up to 3 months.

Makes 1 1/2 dozen

very cherry cupcakes

see variations page 49

Maraschino cherries give these cupcakes a wonderful rich flavor.

for the cupcakes
1 cup (2 sticks) sweet butter, softened
1 cup granulated sugar
2 cups cake flour
2 tsp. baking powder
1 tsp. salt
4 large eggs
1/2 cup buttermilk
2 tbsp. kirsch

for the frosting
3 cups confectioners' sugar, sifted
1 cup (2 sticks) sweet butter
Pinch of salt
Red food coloring
18 bottled morello or maraschino cherries
    with stems

Preheat the oven to 350°F (175°C). Place 18 paper baking cups in muffin pans.

Combine all the cupcake ingredients in a large bowl and beat with an electric mixer until smooth, about 2 to 3 minutes. Spoon the batter into the cups. Bake for 20 to 22 minutes. Remove pans from the oven and cool for 5 minutes. Then remove the cupcakes and cool on a rack. To make the frosting, beat the confectioners' sugar, butter, and salt in a medium bowl with an electric mixer until smooth. Add a few drops of the food coloring and beat until well combined and pink. Spread the frosting onto the cooled cupcakes and garnish with a cherry.

Store unfrosted in an airtight container for up to 3 days, or freeze for up to 3 months.

Makes 1 1/2 dozen

classic chocolate buttercream cupcakes

see variations page 50

The semisweet chocolate in this recipe gives the frosting a wonderful glossy sheen.

for the cupcakes
1 cup (2 sticks) sweet butter, softened
1 cup granulated sugar
1 1/2 cups cake flour
1 1/2 tsp. baking powder
4 tbsp. Dutch-process cocoa powder
4 large eggs
1/2 cup buttermilk
1 tsp. vanilla extract

for the frosting
1 1/2 cups (10 1/2 oz.) chopped semisweet
    chocolate
2 tbsp. heavy cream
1/2 cup (1 stick) sweet butter, softened
1 1/2 cups confectioners' sugar, sifted

Preheat the oven to 350°F (175°C). Place 18 paper baking cups in muffin pans. Combine all the cupcake ingredients in a large bowl and beat with an electric mixer until smooth, about 2 to 3 minutes. Spoon the batter into the cups. Bake for 20 to 22 minutes or until a cake tester inserted in the center comes out clean. Remove pans from the oven and cool for 5 minutes. Then remove the cupcakes and cool on a rack. For the frosting, put the chocolate, cream, and butter in a pan over low heat. Stir gently until combined. Remove from the heat and stir in the confectioners' sugar until the mixture is smooth. Swirl onto the cupcakes.

Store unfrosted in an airtight container for up to 2 days.

Makes 1 1/2 dozen

applesauce & cinnamon cupcakes

see variations page 51

Cinnamon brings a delicate sweetness to this cupcake recipe and complements the applesauce marvelously.

1/2 cup (1 stick) sweet butter, softened
1/2 cup plus 1 tbsp. granulated sugar
1 cup cake flour
1 tsp. baking powder
1/2 tsp. salt
2 large eggs
1/4 cup buttermilk

3/4 cup unsweetened applesauce
3/4 tsp. cinnamon
1/2 cup (3 1/2 oz.) chopped pecans
1/2 cup (3 1/2 oz.) golden raisins
1 small red eating apple, thinly sliced
2 tbsp. granulated sugar

Preheat the oven to 350°F (175°C). Grease a 12-cup muffin pan. Place the butter, sugar, flour, baking powder, salt, eggs, and buttermilk in a bowl and beat with an electric mixer until smooth and pale, about 2 to 3 minutes. Stir in the applesauce, cinnamon, pecans, and raisins.

Spoon the batter into the cups. Lay the apple slices on top and sprinkle with a little sugar.

Bake for 25 to 27 minutes. Remove pan from the oven and cool for 5 minutes. Then remove the cupcakes and cool on a rack. Serve warm.

Store in an airtight container for up to 3 days, or freeze for up to 3 months.

Makes 1 dozen

peanut butter cupcakes

see variations page 52

The texture of crunchy peanut butter in this recipe is excellent, though creamier varieties also work.

for the cupcakes
1 cup (2 sticks) sweet butter, softened
1 cup granulated sugar
2 cups cake flour
2 tsp. baking powder
1 tsp. salt
4 large eggs
1/2 cup buttermilk
1 cup crunchy peanut butter

for the frosting
1/2 cup crunchy peanut butter
1/2 cup (1 stick) sweet butter, softened
2 tsp. vanilla extract
2 cups confectioners' sugar, sifted
2 tbsp. milk

Preheat the oven to 350°F (175°C). Place 18 paper baking cups in muffin pans. Combine the butter, sugar, flour, baking powder, salt, eggs, and buttermilk in a large bowl and beat with an electric mixer until smooth, about 2 to 3 minutes. Stir in the peanut butter until well combined. Spoon the batter into the cups. Bake for 20 to 22 minutes. Remove pans from the oven and cool for 5 minutes. Then remove the cupcakes and cool on a rack.

To make the frosting, combine the peanut butter, butter, and vanilla in a medium bowl. Using an electric mixer, beat until light and fluffy, about 1 to 2 minutes. Add the confectioners' sugar along with the milk, and beat until well combined. Swirl the frosting onto the cooled cupcakes. Store unfrosted in an airtight container for up to 3 days, or freeze for up to 3 months.

Makes 1 1/2 dozen

poppy seed cupcakes with lemon drizzle

see variations page 53

The poppy seeds give these cupcakes a wonderful crunch!

for the cupcakes
1 cup (2 sticks) sweet butter, softened
1 cup granulated sugar
2 cups cake flour
2 tsp. baking powder
1 tsp. salt
4 large eggs
1/2 cup buttermilk
1 tsp. vanilla extract

1 tbsp. poppy seeds
1 tbsp. grated lemon zest

for the drizzle
1 cup confectioners' sugar
4 tbsp. lemon juice
2 tbsp. poppy seeds

Preheat the oven to 350°F (175°C). Place 18 paper baking cups in muffin pans. Combine the butter, sugar, flour, baking powder, salt, eggs, and buttermilk in a large bowl and beat with an electric mixer until smooth, about 2 to 3 minutes. Stir in the vanilla, poppy seeds, and lemon zest until well combined. Spoon the batter into the cups. Bake for 20 to 22 minutes. Remove pans from the oven and cool for 5 minutes. Then remove the cupcakes and cool on a rack. To make the drizzle, sift the confectioners' sugar into a bowl and stir in the lemon juice until it resembles the consistency of heavy cream. Stir in the poppy seeds and drizzle over the cupcakes.

Store in an airtight container for up to 2 days, or freeze for up to 3 months.

Makes 1 1/2 dozen

madeleines

see variations page 54

These light, shell-shaped cupcakes hail from the town of Commercy in the Lorraine region of France.

for the madeleines
4 large eggs
1 cup granulated sugar
1 cup all-purpose flour
1 tsp. baking powder
1 tbsp. grated lemon zest
1/2 cup (1 stick) sweet butter, melted
   and cooled

for the drizzle
1 cup confectioners' sugar
4 tbsp. lemon juice
1 tbsp. grated orange zest

Preheat the oven to 350°F (175°C). Grease a pan for 18 small madeleines. In a medium bowl, beat the eggs and sugar until pale and thick. Sift the flour and baking powder into a separate medium bowl. Slowly add the flour to the egg mixture. Stir in the lemon zest, and pour in the melted butter. Refrigerate for 20 minutes. Spoon the batter into the pan, filling each mold about two-thirds full. Bake for 20 minutes. Remove pan from the oven and cool for 10 minutes. Then remove the madeleines and cool on a rack.

To make the drizzle, sift the confectioners' sugar into a bowl and stir in the lemon juice until it resembles the consistency of heavy cream. Stir in the orange zest and drizzle over the madeleines, before dusting with confectioners' sugar. Store in an airtight container up to 2 days, or freeze for up to 3 months.

Makes 1 1/2 dozen

banana cupcakes

see variations page 55

The subtle flavor of banana perfectly complements the cream cheese frosting.

for the cupcakes
1 cup (2 sticks) sweet butter, softened
1 cup granulated sugar
2 cups cake flour
2 tsp. baking powder
1 tsp. salt
4 large eggs
1/2 cup buttermilk
1/4 tsp. nutmeg
1 cup (about 2 large) mashed ripe bananas

for the frosting
1 cup cream cheese
1 1/2 cups confectioners' sugar, sifted
1 tbsp. lemon juice
1 tsp. vanilla extract
1 banana, thinly sliced

Preheat the oven to 350°F (175°C). Place 18 paper baking cups in muffin pans. Combine the butter, sugar, flour, baking powder, salt, eggs, buttermilk, and nutmeg in a large bowl and beat with an electric mixer until smooth, about 2 to 3 minutes. Stir in the mashed bananas until well combined. Spoon the batter into the cups. Bake for 20 to 22 minutes. Remove pans from the oven and cool for 5 minutes. Then remove the cupcakes and cool on a rack.

To make the frosting, slowly beat the cream cheese in a large bowl with an electric mixer until it is soft and smooth. Add the confectioners' sugar, lemon juice, and vanilla. Beat briskly until smooth and well combined. Swirl the frosting onto the cooled cupcakes. Decorate each cupcake with a banana slice. Store unfrosted in an airtight container for up to 3 days, or freeze for up to 3 months.

Makes 1 1/2 dozen

variations

spanish orange syrup cupcakes

see base recipe page 19

blood orange syrup cupcakes
Prepare the basic cupcake recipe, substituting blood oranges for the sweet oranges.

orange & lemon syrup cupcakes
Prepare the basic cupcake recipe, adding 2 tablespoons lemon juice to the orange purée. For the syrup, zest 1 medium lemon and add with the orange zest to the water and sugar syrup.

grapefruit & orange syrup cupcakes
Prepare the basic cupcake recipe. Add 2 tablespoons grapefruit juice to the orange purée. For the syrup, zest half a medium grapefruit and add it with the orange zest to the water and sugar syrup.

key lime syrup cupcakes
Prepare the basic cupcake recipe, substituting 6 small Key limes or 4 Persian limes for the sweet oranges, and use lime rind to make the syrup.

mandarin oranges & almond syrup cupcakes
Prepare the basic cupcake recipe, substituting 1/2 cup (4 oz.) puréed mandarin oranges for the oranges in the cupcakes and prepared almond syrup for the orange syrup.

variations

vanilla cupcakes

see base recipe page 21

saffron cupcakes
Prepare the basic cupcake recipe. Add a pinch of saffron to 2 tablespoons boiling water. Infuse for 5 minutes. After creaming the cupcake ingredients, stir in saffron and water.

almond cupcakes
Prepare the basic cupcake recipe, adding 3 tablespoons ground almonds to the mixture and substituting 1 teaspoon almond extract for the vanilla extract.

vanilla & raisin cupcakes
Prepare the basic cupcake recipe. After creaming the cupcake ingredients, stir in 1/2 cup (3 1/2 oz.) golden raisins.

coffeetime cupcakes
Prepare the basic cupcake recipe, substituting coffee extract for vanilla.

gingerbread pots

see base recipe page 22

fruity pots
Fold 1/2 cup (3 1/2 oz.) mixed chopped dried apricots, raisins, and golden raisins into the egg mixture before stirring into the dry ingredients.

rhubarb ginger pots
Add 1/2 cup (3 1/2 oz.) cooked sweetened rhubarb to the egg mixture before stirring in the dry ingredients.

banana ginger pots
Add 1 mashed banana to the egg mixture before stirring in the dry ingredients.

apple ginger pots
Add 1 grated Golden Delicious apple to the egg mixture before stirring in the dry ingredients.

gingerbread pots with ginger honey drizzle
Prepare the basic cupcake recipe, substituting 1/2 cup (6 oz.) honey and 1 tablespoon freshly grated ginger for the drizzle. Simmer the honey and ginger together in a saucepan for 5 minutes, let cool, then drizzle over the cupcakes.

lemon butterfly cupcakes

see base recipe page 24

orange & lemon butterfly cupcakes
Prepare the basic cupcake recipe. Add 1 1/2 tablespoons grated orange zest to the frosting mixture.

red currant butterfly cupcakes
Prepare the basic cupcake recipe. Lightly crush 1/3 cup (2 1/2 oz.) fresh or thawed frozen red currants with a fork and add to the frosting mixture.

hazelnut & raisin butterfly cupcakes
Prepare the basic cupcake recipe. Stir 3 tablespoons roughly chopped toasted hazelnuts and 2 tablespoons golden raisins into the creamed frosting mixture.

blueberry & lemon butterfly cupcakes
Prepare the basic cupcake recipe, adding 1/2 cup (3 1/2 oz.) dried blueberries.

rum & raisin cupcakes

see base recipe page 26

orange liqueur & candied peel cupcakes
Prepare the basic cupcake recipe, substituting orange liqueur for the rum and 1/2 cup (3 1/2 oz.) chopped candied peel for the raisins.

vodka, chili & chocolate chip cupcakes
Prepare the basic cupcake recipe. Substitute vodka for the rum. Add 1 tablespoon seeded and finely chopped chilies and 1/2 cup (3 1/2 oz.) semisweet chocolate chips in place of the raisins.

malibu & pineapple cupcakes
Prepare the basic cupcake recipe, substituting Malibu for the rum and 1/2 cup (3 1/2 oz.) finely chopped dried pineapple for the raisins.

golden sherry cupcakes
Prepare the basic cupcake recipe, substituting sherry for the rum and 1/2 cup (2 1/2 oz.) golden raisins for the raisins.

mini raspberry & coconut cupcakes

see base recipe page 29

mini blueberry & coconut cupcakes
Prepare the basic cupcake recipe, substituting blueberries for the raspberries and adding 1 tablespoon finely grated lime zest.

mini blackberry & coconut cupcakes
Prepare the basic cupcake recipe, substituting 1/2 cup (2 1/2 oz.) blackberries for the raspberries.

mini lime, mango & coconut cupcakes
Prepare the basic cupcake recipe, substituting 1/2 cup (2 oz.) finely chopped fresh or frozen mango and 1 tablespoon finely grated lime zest for the raspberries.

mini pistachio & apricot cupcakes
Prepare the basic cupcake recipe, substituting ground pistachios for the almond meal and chopped, canned apricots for the raspberries.

variations

carrot & walnut cupcakes

see base recipe page 30

coffee & walnut-frosted carrot cupcakes
Prepare the basic cupcake recipe. Add 1 teaspoon hot coffee, 1 teaspoon instant coffee granules, and 1 teaspoon coffee liqueur to the frosting mixture. Swirl the coffee frosting on top of the cupcakes, and garnish with chopped walnuts.

orange cream cheese-frosted carrot cupcakes
Prepare the basic cupcake recipe. To make the frosting, substitute 1 tablespoon orange juice for the lemon juice. Swirl the frosting and garnish with chopped walnuts and finely grated lemon zest.

mascarpone-frosted carrot cupcakes
Prepare the basic cupcake recipe. To make the frosting, substitute 1 cup (8 oz.) mascarpone for the cream cheese.

zucchini, yellow squash & carrot cupcakes
Prepare the basic cupcake recipe, using 1/3 cup (2 oz.) each of shredded carrots, grated zucchini, and grated yellow squash in place of carrots.

very cherry cupcakes

see base recipe page 31

chocolate chip & cherry-frosted cupcakes
Prepare the basic cupcake recipe. Stir 1/2 cup (3 1/2 oz.) semisweet chocolate chips into the frosting mixture after adding the food coloring.

almond & cherry-frosted cupcakes
Prepare the basic cupcake recipe, adding 3 tablespoons ground almonds to the batter mixture. Sprinkle 2 tablespoons of toasted almonds on top of the frosting, and garnish each with a cherry.

crispy meringue & cherry-frosted cupcakes
Prepare the basic cupcake recipe. Place 4 small meringue shells in a plastic food storage bag and lightly crush them with a rolling pin. Gently stir into the frosting mixture after adding the food coloring. Swirl onto the cupcakes.

cherry, cherry cupcakes
Prepare the basic cupcake recipe, adding 1/2 cup (2 1/2 oz.) dried cherries to the batter.

variations

classic chocolate buttercream cupcakes

see base recipe page 32

white & semisweet chocolate buttercream cupcakes
Prepare the basic cupcake recipe, stirring 3 tablespoons mixed semisweet chocolate chips and white chocolate chips into the creamed batter.

macadamia nut-frosted buttercream cupcakes
Prepare the basic cupcake recipe. Lightly toast 1/2 cup (3 1/2 oz.) macadamia nuts and chop finely. Stir the macadamia nuts into the frosting mixture after adding the sugar.

orange & semisweet chocolate buttercream cupcakes
Prepare the basic cupcake recipe, substituting 1 tablespoon orange zest for the vanilla extract.

mocha buttercream cupcakes
Prepare the basic cupcake recipe. For the frosting, substitute 1 tablespoon freshly brewed dark coffee for 1 tablespoon of cream.

sour cream chocolate cupcakes
Prepare the basic cupcake recipe, substituting sour cream for the buttermilk in the cupcakes.

applesauce & cinnamon cupcakes

see base recipe page 34

applesauce & pear cupcakes

Prepare the basic cupcake recipe. Substitute 1 ripe and firm, medium pear for the apple. Lay slices on top of each cupcake and sprinkle with sugar.

applesauce & warm caramel cupcakes

Prepare the basic cupcake recipe. To make a caramel topping, place 2 cups (6 oz.) caramels in a medium pan with 3 tablespoons evaporated milk. Heat gently, stirring until all the caramels have melted. Prick the top of the cupcakes with a toothpick and spoon the melted caramel over the cooled cakes. Then lay slices of apple on top of each cupcake.

applesauce & brandy drizzle cupcakes

Prepare the basic cupcake recipe. To make the drizzle, combine 4 tablespoons apple brandy with 3 tablespoons sugar in a medium pan. Simmer gently for 5 minutes, then spoon over the cupcakes. Then lay slices of apple on top of each cupcake.

variations

peanut butter cupcakes

see base recipe page 36

peanut butter & jam cupcakes
Prepare the basic cupcake recipe. When the cupcakes have cooled, use a sharp knife to slice off the tops. Using a teaspoon, hollow out a small hole in the top of each cupcake. Spoon 1/2 teaspoon strawberry or raspberry jam into the small hole. Place the top back on the cupcake and frost.

chocolate peanut butter cupcakes
Prepare the basic cupcake recipe. Add 1/2 cup (3 1/2 oz.) semisweet chocolate chips to the batter.

peanut butter cupcakes with fudge frosting
Prepare the basic cupcake recipe. For the frosting, substitute smooth peanut butter for the crunchy. Add 2 tablespoons Dutch-process cocoa powder to the frosting mixture after adding the milk.

peanut butter bar cupcakes
Prepare the basic cupcake recipe. When the cupcakes have cooled, use a sharp knife to slice off the tops. Using a teaspoon, hollow out a small hole in the top of each cupcake. Spoon 1/2 teaspoon chopped peanut candy bar into the small hole. Place the top back on the cupcake and frost.

poppy seed cupcakes with lemon drizzle

see base recipe page 37

poppy seed cupcakes with orange & lemon drizzle
Prepare the basic cupcake recipe using 1/2 tablespoon orange zest and
1/2 tablespoon lemon zest. To make the drizzle, use 2 tablespoons lemon
juice and 2 tablespoons orange juice.

poppy seed & blueberry cupcakes with lime drizzle
Prepare the basic cupcake recipe. After creaming the batter, stir in 1/2 cup
(2 oz.) blueberries, and substitute 1 tablespoon finely grated lime zest for the
lemon zest.

poppy seed & cranberry cupcakes with lemon drizzle
Prepare the basic cupcake recipe. After creaming the batter, stir in 1/2 cup
(3 1/2 oz.) dried chopped cranberries.

almond poppy seed cupcakes with almond drizzle
Prepare the basic cupcake recipe, substituting 1 teaspoon almond extract for
the lemon zest. For the drizzle, substitute 1 teaspoon almond extract plus
3 tablespoons milk in place of the lemon juice.

variations

madeleines

see base recipe page 39

cassis-drizzled madeleines
Prepare the basic recipe. For the drizzle, substitute 4 tablespoons cassis liqueur for the lemon juice, and proceed as in base recipe.

chocolate madeleines
Prepare the basic recipe. Substitute 2 tablespoons Dutch-process cocoa powder for 2 tablespoons of the flour.

vanilla madeleines
Prepare the basic recipe. Add 1 teaspoon vanilla extract to the eggs and sugar before creaming the batter. For the drizzle, mix 1 cup (4 1/2 oz.) confectioners' sugar, 4 tablespoons milk, 1/2 teaspoon vanilla extract until it resembles the consistency of heavy cream. Proceed as in base recipe.

orange madeleines
Prepare the basic cupcake recipe, substituting orange zest for lemon.

banana cupcakes

see base recipe page 40

chocolate chip & banana cupcakes
Prepare the basic cupcake recipe. Stir in 1/2 cup (3 1/2 oz.) semisweet chocolate chips along with the mashed bananas.

cinnamon & oat-topped banana cupcakes
Prepare the basic cupcake recipe, omitting the frosting. Place 3 tablespoons granulated sugar, 1 teaspoon cinnamon, 2 tablespoons softened sweet butter, 4 tablespoons rolled oats, and 1 tablespoon flour in a medium bowl. Mix until well combined. Sprinkle a little over the cupcakes before baking them.

walnut & cinnamon-frosted banana cupcakes
Prepare the basic cupcake recipe. Add 3 tablespoons chopped walnuts and 1 teaspoon cinnamon to the frosting after creaming it.

blueberry & banana cupcakes
Prepare the basic cupcake recipe. Stir in 1/2 cup (3 oz.) dried blueberries along with the mashed bananas.

fragrant &
spiced cupcakes

Exotic and unexpected flavors make these cupcakes

a culinary adventure. Unusual pairings — pistachio

and rosewater, fig and vanilla, cardamom and

orange — abound.

carnation cupcakes

see variations page 72

Cooking with flowers goes back centuries. You can find old recipes for flower water, jellies, jams, and yes, cupcakes!

for the cupcakes
1 cup (2 sticks) sweet butter, softened
1 cup granulated sugar
2 cups cake flour
2 tsp. baking powder
1 tsp. salt
4 large eggs
1/2 cup buttermilk
1 tsp. vanilla extract

for the frosting
1 3/4 cups confectioners' sugar
2 tbsp. lemon juice
3 dozen red, pink, or striped carnations

Preheat the oven to 350°F (175°C). Place 18 paper baking cups in muffin pans. Combine all the cupcake ingredients in a large bowl and beat with an electric mixer until smooth and pale, about 2 to 3 minutes. Spoon the batter into the cups. Bake for 20 minutes. Remove pans from the oven and cool for 5 minutes. Then remove the cupcakes and cool on a rack.

To make the frosting, sift the confectioners' sugar into a medium bowl. Slowly add the lemon juice, stirring until the frosting holds its shape. Spread the frosting onto the cooled cupcakes. Snip the heels off the carnation flowers and place a flower in the center of each cupcake.

Store unfrosted in an airtight container for up to 3 days, or freeze in an airtight container for up to 3 months.

Makes 1 1/2 dozen

chai cupcakes

see variations page 73

Chai is a spiced Indian tea made with frothy warm milk — almost like an Indian cappuccino! This cupcake captures its light, spicy flavor.

for the cupcakes
2 cups cake flour
1 tsp. baking powder
1/2 tsp. salt
1 tbsp. chai tea powder
1/4 cup (1/2 stick) sweet butter, softened
3/4 cup packed light brown sugar
2 large egg whites
2/3 cup buttermilk

for the frosting
1 cup cream cheese, softened
1 1/2 cups confectioners' sugar, sifted
1 tbsp. lemon juice
1 tsp. vanilla extract

Preheat the oven to 350°F (175°C). Place 12 baking cups in a muffin pan. In a medium bowl, mix the flour, baking powder, salt, and chai powder. In a separate bowl, beat the butter and sugar until smooth. Add the egg whites slowly, beating well. Slowly add the flour mixture, and finally the buttermilk. Mix until combined. Spoon the batter into the cups. Bake for 20 minutes. Remove pan from the oven and cool for 5 minutes. Then remove the cupcakes and cool on a rack. To make the frosting, mix the cream cheese and confectioners' sugar together in a medium bowl and beat until soft and light. Add the lemon and vanilla, and beat until smooth. Spoon the frosting over the cupcakes.

Store unfrosted in an airtight container for up to 3 days, or freeze for up to 3 months.

Makes 1 dozen

fennel cupcakes

see variations page 74

Lightly crushed fennel seeds give this cupcake a sweet licorice flavor. In India, fennel seeds are chewed after meals to refresh the breath.

for the cupcakes
1 cup (2 sticks) sweet butter, softened
1 cup granulated sugar
2 cups cake flour
2 tsp. baking powder
1 tsp. salt
4 large eggs
1/2 cup buttermilk
1 tsp. finely crushed fennel seeds

for the frosting
1 cup cream cheese, softened
1 1/2 cups confectioners' sugar, sifted
1 tbsp. licorice-flavored liqueur
1 tsp. vanilla extract
1 tsp. lightly crushed fennel seeds

Preheat the oven to 350°F (175°C). Place 18 paper baking cups in muffin pans. Combine all the cupcake ingredients in a medium bowl and beat with an electric mixer until smooth and pale, about 2 to 3 minutes. Spoon the batter into the cups. Bake for 20 minutes. Remove pans from the oven and cool for 5 minutes. Then remove the cupcakes and cool on a rack.

To make the frosting, combine the cream cheese and confectioners' sugar, and beat briskly until soft and creamy. Add the liqueur and vanilla, and stir well. Swirl onto the top of the cupcakes, and decorate with the fennel seeds.

Store unfrosted for up to 3 days in an airtight container, or freeze for 3 months.

Makes 1 1/2 dozen

rhubarb & ginger cupcakes

see variations page 75

The combination of rhubarb and ginger is magnificent. It is believed that rhubarb originated in China, where it was used for its medicinal properties.

for the cupcakes
1 cup (2 sticks) sweet butter, softened
1 cup granulated sugar
2 cups cake flour
2 tsp. baking powder
1 tsp. salt
4 large eggs
1/2 cup buttermilk
1 tsp. vanilla
1 cup cooked rhubarb

for the frosting
1 cup cream cheese, softened
1 1/2 cups confectioners' sugar, sifted
1 tbsp. lime juice
1/2 tsp. ground ginger
1 1/2 tbsp. roughly chopped candied ginger

Preheat the oven to 400°F (200°C). Place 18 paper baking cups in muffin pans. Combine all the cupcake ingredients, except the rhubarb, in a medium bowl and beat with an electric mixer until smooth and pale, about 2 to 3 minutes. Spoon the batter into the cups. Bake for 20 minutes. Remove pans from the oven and cool for 5 minutes. Then remove the cupcakes and cool on a rack. Hollow out a small hole in each cake and fill with 1 teaspoon rhubarb.

For the frosting, combine the cream cheese and confectioners' sugar, and beat briskly until soft and creamy. Add the lime juice, ground ginger, and candied ginger and mix well. Spoon onto the cupcakes. Store unfrosted in an airtight container for up to 3 days, or freeze for up to 3 months.

Makes 1 1/2 dozen

lavender & honey cupcakes

see variations page 76

The marriage of lavender and honey is truly wonderful. If you can find lavender honey, it will enhance the flavor even more.

for the cupcakes
1 cup (2 sticks) sweet butter, softened
1 cup granulated sugar
2 cups cake flour
2 tsp. baking powder
1 tsp. salt
4 large eggs
1/2 cup buttermilk
1 tsp. vanilla extract

for the frosting
1 cup cream cheese, softened
1 1/2 cups confectioners' sugar, sifted
1/3 cup honey
Blue food coloring
2 tbsp. dried lavender flowers

Preheat the oven to 350°F (200°C). Place 18 baking cups in muffin pans. Combine all the cupcake ingredients in a medium bowl and beat with an electric mixer until smooth and pale, about 2 to 3 minutes. Spoon the batter into the cups. Bake for 20 minutes. Remove pans from the oven and cool for 5 minutes. Then remove the cupcakes and cool on a rack.

For the frosting, beat the cream cheese and confectioners' sugar in a medium bowl with an electric mixer, until light and creamy. Beat in the honey and a few drops of the food coloring. Stir in half of the lavender flowers. Spread the frosting onto the cupcakes and sprinkle with the reserved lavender flowers.

Store without frosting in an airtight container for up to 3 days, or freeze for up to 3 months.

Makes 1 1/2 dozen

hummingbird cupcakes
with marmalade frosting

see variations page 77

The hummingbird cake is a classic recipe from the American South.

for the cupcakes
1 1/4 cups all-purpose flour
1 tsp. baking powder
1/2 tsp. cinnamon
1/2 tsp. salt
3/4 cup granulated sugar
1/2 cup vegetable oil
2 large eggs
1/2 cup (2 medium) mashed bananas
1 1/2 tbsp. grated orange zest

1/2 cup shredded carrot
1/2 cup crushed pineapple, drained
1/2 cup flaked coconut

for the frosting
1/2 cup (1 stick) sweet butter, softened
2 1/2 cups confectioners' sugar, sifted
2 tbsp. freshly squeezed orange juice
2 tbsp. orange marmalade

Preheat the oven to 350°F (175°C). Place 12 baking cups in a muffin pan. In a medium bowl, sift the flour, baking powder, cinnamon, and salt. In a large bowl, cream the sugar and oil with an electric mixer until light and fluffy. Beat in the eggs slowly, then stir in the dry ingredients in 3 batches. Add the rest of the ingredients, and stir until combined. Spoon the batter into the cups. Bake for 25 minutes. Remove pan from the oven and cool for 5 minutes. Then remove the cupcakes and cool on a rack. To make the frosting, beat the butter in a medium bowl. Add the sugar and orange juice, and beat smooth. Add marmalade or save for garnish. Spread or dollop frosting onto cupcakes and garnish with marmalade if desired. Store unfrosted in an airtight container for up to 3 days, or freeze for up to 3 months.

Makes 1 dozen

pistachio & rosewater cupcakes

see variations page 78

Rosewater is a delicate, sweet flavoring made by steeping rose petals in water, oil, or alcohol. Try to use unsalted pistachios in this recipe.

for the cupcakes
1 cup (2 sticks) sweet butter, softened
1 cup granulated sugar
2 cups cake flour
2 tsp. baking powder
1 tsp. salt
4 large eggs
1/2 cup buttermilk
1 tsp. rosewater

for the frosting
1 cup cream cheese
1 1/2 cups confectioners' sugar, sifted
2 tbsp. rosewater
3 tbsp. chopped pistachios

Preheat the oven to 350°F (175°C). Place 18 paper baking cups in muffin pans. Combine all the cupcake ingredients in a medium bowl and beat with an electric mixer until smooth and pale, about 2 to 3 minutes. Spoon the batter into the cups. Bake for 20 minutes. Remove pans from the oven and cool for 5 minutes. Then remove the cupcakes and cool on a rack.

For the frosting, combine the cream cheese and confectioners' sugar, and beat with an electric mixer until soft and creamy. Add the rosewater and stir well. Add pistachios, or save them for garnish. Swirl frosting onto the top of the cupcakes and garnish with pistachios if desired. Store without frosting for up to 3 days in an airtight container, or freeze for up to 3 months.

Makes 1 1/2 dozen

orange & armagnac cupcakes

see variations page 79

For adults only! These cupcakes would be ideal on a cold winter night.

for the cupcakes
1 cup (2 sticks) sweet butter, softened
1 cup granulated sugar
2 cups cake flour
2 tsp. baking powder
1 tsp. salt
4 large eggs
1/4 cup buttermilk
2 tbsp. Armagnac

for the frosting
1 cup cream cheese, softened
1 1/2 cups confectioners' sugar, sifted
1 tsp. orange extract
1 1/2 tbsp. grated orange zest

Preheat the oven to 350°F (175°C). Place 18 paper baking cups in muffin pans. Combine all the cupcake ingredients in a medium bowl and beat with an electric mixer until smooth and pale, about 2 to 3 minutes. Spoon the batter into the cups. Bake for 20 minutes. Remove pans from the oven and cool for 5 minutes.

With a skewer or toothpick, poke holes in the tops of the cupcakes, then drizzle lightly with Armagnac. Then remove the cupcakes and cool on a rack. To make the frosting, beat the cream cheese in a bowl with an electric mixer until light and fluffy. Beat in the confectioners' sugar for 1 to 2 minutes, then beat in the orange extract and zest until smooth and light. Spread the frosting on the cupcakes. Store unfrosted for up to 2 days in an airtight container, or freeze for up to 3 months.

Makes 1 1/2 dozen

spiced sour cream cupcakes

see variations page 80

The hearty flavor of these cupcakes is perfect for tailgating parties and fall picnics.

for the cupcakes
1 1/2 cups all-purpose flour
1 tsp. baking powder
2 tsp. cinnamon
1 tsp. allspice
1/4 tsp. nutmeg
2 large eggs
3/4 cup sour cream
1 cup packed light brown sugar

3 tbsp. golden raisins
3 tbsp. chopped pecans

for the frosting
1 cup cream cheese, softened
1/2 cup (1 stick) sweet butter, softened
1 1/2 cups confectioners' sugar, sifted
1 tbsp. grated orange zest
2 tbsp. orange juice

Preheat the oven to 350°F (175°C). Place 18 paper baking cups in muffin pans. Sift the dry ingredients into a medium bowl and put aside. In a large bowl, beat the eggs and sour cream with an electric mixer. Add the sugar and mix well. Then add the dry ingredients in 3 batches, and mix until smooth. Stir in the raisins and pecans. Spoon the batter into the cups.

Bake for 20 minutes until firm. Remove pans from the oven and cool for 5 minutes. Then remove the cupcakes and cool on a rack. To make the frosting, beat the cream cheese and butter together with an electric mixer, until light and fluffy. Add the confectioners' sugar and beat until creamy. Beat in the orange zest and the juice. Spread the frosting on the cupcakes.

Store unfrosted in an airtight container for up to 3 days, or freeze for up to 3 months.

Makes 1 1/2 dozen

cardamom & orange cupcakes

see variations page 81

Cardamom has a pungent aroma and is often used in Indian cooking to flavor curries.

for the cupcakes
1 cup (2 sticks) sweet butter, softened
1 cup granulated sugar
2 cups cake flour
2 tsp. baking powder
1 tsp. salt
4 large eggs
1/2 cup buttermilk
1 tsp. ground cardamom
1 tsp. orange extract

for the frosting
2 cups confectioners' sugar, sifted
1/2 cup (1 stick) sweet butter, softened
1/4 cup sour cream
1 1/2 tbsp. grated orange zest
1 tsp. orange extract
36 cardamom pods (for decoration only)

Preheat the oven to 350°F (175°C). Place 18 paper baking cups in muffin pans. Combine all the cupcake ingredients in a medium bowl and beat with an electric mixer until smooth and pale, about 2 to 3 minutes. Spoon the batter into the cups. Bake in the oven for 20 minutes. Remove pans from the oven and cool for 5 minutes. Then remove the cupcakes and cool on a rack.

To make the frosting, beat the confectioners' sugar, butter, sour cream, orange zest, and orange extract with an electric mixer until smooth. Spread the frosting on the cupcakes and top each with 2 cardamom pods. Store unfrosted for up to 2 days in an airtight container, or freeze for up to 3 months.

Makes 1 1/2 dozen

variations

carnation cupcakes

see base recipe page 57

frosted flower cupcakes
Prepare the basic cupcake recipe. To prepare the frosted flowers, put an
egg white in a small bowl and some granulated sugar in another small bowl.
Take a selection of flower petals (roses and pansies work well) and brush
with egg white on both sides. Dust the petals with the sugar, place on a
tray, and leave in a cool dry place to dry and stiffen. Lay on top of the
frosted cupcakes.

rose cupcakes
Prepare the basic cupcake recipe. Substitute 2 dozen rose petals for the
carnations.

citrus cream carnation cupcakes
Prepare the basic cupcake recipe. To make a citrus cream frosting, combine
1/2 cup (4 oz.) cream cheese with 2 teaspoons orange and lemon zest in a
small bowl. Stir in 3 tablespoons confectioners' sugar, spread onto the
cupcakes, and garnish with the carnations.

jordan almond cupcakes
Prepare the basic cupcake recipe, substituting almond extract for vanilla.
Substitute pastel coated Jordan almonds for the carnations.

variations

chai cupcakes

see base recipe page 58

chocolate chip & chai cupcakes
Prepare the basic cupcake recipe, stirring in 1/2 cup (3 1/2 oz.) semisweet chocolate chips after adding the buttermilk.

cinnamon & orange chai cupcakes
Prepare the basic cupcake recipe, adding 2 teaspoons cinnamon to the dry ingredients. Add 1 tablespoon grated orange zest along with the buttermilk.

white chocolate & vanilla chai cupcakes
Prepare the basic cupcake recipe. Add 1/2 cup (3 1/2 oz.) white chocolate chips and 1 teaspoon vanilla extract after adding the buttermilk.

chai cupcakes with lemon drizzle
Prepare the basic cupcake recipe. Omit the cream cheese and whisk the confectioners' sugar, lemon juice, and vanilla together and drizzle over the cupcakes.

malted milk cupcakes
Prepare the basic cupcake recipe, substituting malted milk powder for the chai. For the frosting, substitute 2 tablespoons chocolate syrup for the lemon juice and decorate the cupcakes with chocolate-covered malted milk balls.

variations

fennel cupcakes

see base recipe page 60

fennel & orange cupcakes
Prepare the basic cupcake recipe. Add 1 tablespoon finely grated orange zest to the cupcake mixture. For the frosting, substitute 1 teaspoon orange extract for the vanilla.

fennel & almond cupcakes
Prepare the basic cupcake recipe, adding 4 tablespoons chopped blanched almonds after mixing the cupcake batter.

fennel & pink pepper cupcakes
Prepare the basic cupcake recipe. For the frosting, omit the vanilla extract and instead add 1 teaspoon finely crushed pink peppercorns.

cardamom cupcakes
Prepare the basic cupcake recipe, substituting crushed cardamom seeds for the fennel and orange-flavored liqueur for the licorice-flavored liqueur.

poppy seed & amaretto cupcakes
Prepare the basic cupcake recipe, substituting poppy seeds for the fennel and almond-flavored liqueur for the licorice-flavored liqueur.

rhubarb & ginger cupcakes

see base recipe page 61

rhubarb, cinnamon & ginger cupcakes
Prepare the basic cupcake recipe. Add 2 teaspoons cinnamon to the cupcake
mixture before stirring the batter.

rhubarb, custard & ginger cupcakes
Prepare the basic cupcake recipe. Slice the cupcakes horizontally and spread
1 tablespoon custard (or prepared vanilla pudding) onto the base. Pop the
top back on and smother with the ginger frosting.

golden raisin, rhubarb & ginger cupcakes
Prepare the basic cupcake recipe. After mixing the batter, add 1/4 cup (2 oz.)
golden raisins.

lemony rhubarb cupcakes
Prepare the basic cupcake recipe, substituting lemon zest for the vanilla
extract. In the frosting, substitute lemon juice for lime juice and omit the
ground and candied ginger.

orange rhubarb cupcakes
Prepare the basic cupcake recipe, substituting orange zest for the vanilla
extract. In the frosting, substitute orange juice for lime juice and finely
chopped candied orange peel for the ground and candied ginger.

variations

lavender & honey cupcakes

see base recipe page 63

dark chocolate & lavender cupcakes
Prepare the basic cupcake recipe. After mixing the batter, fold in 1/2 cup (3 1/2 oz.) dark chocolate chips.

lavender blueberry cupcakes
Prepare the basic cupcake recipe, substituting lemon zest for vanilla and adding 1 cup dried blueberries to the cupcake batter after creaming. For the frosting, substitute 2 tablespoons lemon juice for the honey and 1 cup (4 oz.) fresh blueberries for the lavender flowers.

lavender & orange flower cream cupcakes
Prepare the basic cupcake recipe. To make the frosting, combine 3 tablespoons orange flower water with the cream cheese and confectioners' sugar. Add the honey. Beat well and stir in the lavender flowers.

lemon lavender cupcakes
Prepare the basic cupcake recipe, substituting lemon zest for the vanilla extract. To make the frosting, add 1 teaspoon lemon zest to the cream cheese and confectioners' sugar. Add the honey. Beat well and stir in the lavender flowers.

variations

hummingbird cupcakes with marmalade frosting

see base recipe page 64

macadamia hummingbird cupcakes with marmalade frosting
Prepare the basic cupcake recipe adding 1/2 cup (3 1/2 oz.) chopped
macadamia nuts after mixing in the eggs.

hummingbird cupcakes with figs
Prepare the basic cupcake recipe, substituting 1/4 cup (2 oz.) chopped dried
figs for the pineapple.

hummingird cupcakes with lemon frosting
Prepare the basic cupcake recipe. To make the frosting, substitute
2 tablespoons lemon juice for the orange juice, and 2 tablespoons
lemon curd for the marmalade.

hummingbird cupcakes with pineapple frosting
Prepare the basic cupcake recipe. To make the frosting, substitute
2 tablespoons lemon juice for the orange juice, and 1/4 cup (1 1/2 oz.)
crushed pineapple for the marmalade.

black walnut hummingbird cupcakes with marmalade frosting
Prepare the basic cupcake, adding 1/2 cup (2 oz.) finely ground black
walnuts to the batter after creaming.

variations

pistachio & rosewater cupcakes

see base recipe page 67

pomegranate & rosewater cupcakes
Prepare the basic cupcake recipe. For the frosting, add 3 tablespoons pomegranate seeds after combining the cream cheese and confectioners' sugar.

walnut & rosewater cupcakes
Prepare the basic cupcake recipe. For the frosting, substitute 3 tablespoons chopped walnuts for the pistachios.

almond & rosewater cupcakes
Prepare the basic cupcake recipe. For the frosting, substitute 3 tablespoons toasted almonds for the pistachios.

pistachio & orange flower water cupcakes
Prepare the basic cupcake recipe, substituting orange flower water for the rosewater. For the frosting, substitute 1 tablespoon orange flower water for the rosewater.

pistachio & amaretto cupcakes
Prepare the basic cupcake recipe, substituting 1 tablespoon Amaretto for the 1 teaspoon rosewater.

variations

orange & armagnac cupcakes

see base recipe page 68

orange, chocolate chip & armagnac cupcakes

Prepare the basic cupcake recipe, adding 1/2 cup (3 1/2 oz.) semisweet chocolate chips after combining the rest of the cupcake ingredients.

almond & amaretto cupcakes

Prepare the basic cupcake recipe, substituting 2 tablespoons Amaretto for the Armagnac. Add 3 tablespoons ground almonds to the cupcake mixture along with the other ingredients. For the frosting, add 2 tablespoons chopped almonds, and omit the orange juice and zest.

hazelnut & kahlua cupcakes

Prepare the basic cupcake recipe, substituting 2 tablespoons Kahlua for the Armagnac. Add 3 tablespoons finely chopped hazelnuts to the cupcake mixture along with the other ingredients. For the frosting, add 2 tablespoons chopped hazelnuts, and omit the orange juice and zest.

orange, prune & armagnac cupcakes

Prepare the basic cupcake recipe, adding 1/2 cup (3 oz.) chopped, pitted prunes after combining the rest of the cupcake ingredients.

variations

spiced sour cream cupcakes

see base recipe page 69

ginger-frosted spiced sour cream cupcakes
Prepare the basic cupcake recipe. For the frosting, substitute 3 tablespoons chopped candied ginger for the orange zest and orange juice.

coffee-frosted spiced sour cream cupcakes
Prepare the basic cupcake recipe, but omit the frosting. For the frosting, mix 2 tablespoons strong coffee and 2 tablespoons malted milk powder until dissolved. Whisk 1 1/2 cups (10 oz.) confectioners' sugar into the coffee mixture until dissolved.

maple & walnut-frosted spiced sour cream cupcakes
Prepare the basic cupcake recipe. To make the frosting, add 1/2 teaspoon maple-flavored extract to the creamed confectioners' sugar, butter, and cream cheese. Omit the orange juice and zest. Smear the frosting onto the cupcakes and top with 1/2 cup (3 1/2 oz.) chopped walnuts.

applesauce spiced cupcakes
Prepare the basic cupcake recipe, substituting applesauce for the sour cream.

cardamom & orange cupcakes

see base recipe page 70

coffee & cardamom-frosted cupcakes

Prepare the basic cupcake recipe. For the frosting, omit the orange zest
and extract. Add 2 tablespoons instant coffee granules to 1 teaspoon hot
coffee. Stir to dissolve. Stir in 1 tablespoon Kahlua. Set aside to cool. Stir
the cooled coffee mixture into the creamed confectioners' sugar, butter,
and sour cream.

cardamom, custard & orange cupcakes

Prepare the basic cupcake recipe. Slice the cupcakes horizontally and spread
1 tablespoon custard (or prepared vanilla pudding) onto the base. Pop the
top back on and smother with the orange frosting.

cardamom & lemongrass cupcakes

Prepare the basic cupcake recipe. For the frosting, add 1 tablespoon finely
chopped lemongrass after creaming the other ingredients.

cardamom, ice cream & orange cupcakes

Prepare the basic cupcake recipe. Slice the cupcakes horizontally and place a
small scoop of cinnamon ice cream onto the base. Pop the top back on and
drizzle with warm caramel ice cream topping.

chocolate cupcakes

Minted chocolate cupcakes, chocolate chip and

raisin brioches, white chocolate and strawberry

cupcakes — the cupcakes in this chapter will satisfy

your chocolate craving in an instant!

chocolate mud cupcakes

see variations page 103

These cupcakes are so simple to make, you won't hesitate to make another batch!

1 cup (7 oz.) semisweet chocolate chips
1 1/4 cups (2 1/2 sticks) sweet butter
5 large eggs
2/3 cup granulated sugar

3/4 cup cake flour
3/4 tsp. baking powder
1/2 tsp. salt
2 tbsp. Dutch-process cocoa powder, for dusting

Preheat the oven to 325°F (160°C). Place 12 paper baking cups in a muffin pan.

In a double boiler, or a medium bowl set over a pan of gently simmering water, melt the chocolate and butter together, stirring well. Leave to cool a little.

Beat the eggs and sugar in a large bowl until pale and thick. Fold the flour, baking powder, and salt into the egg mixture and then stir in the melted chocolate and butter until well blended.

Spoon the mixture into the cups and bake for 20 minutes. The cupcakes will be soft and gooey in texture and appearance. Remove pan from the oven and cool for 5 minutes. Then remove the cupcakes from pan. Serve swiftly, dusted with cocoa powder.

Store in the refrigerator in an airtight container for up to 3 days.

Makes 1 dozen

chocolate ice cream cupcakes

see variations page 104

It's best to move these cupcakes from freezer to refrigerator 30 minutes before serving.

for the cupcakes
1 cup (2 sticks) sweet butter, softened
1 cup granulated sugar
1 1/2 cups cake flour
4 tbsp. Dutch-process cocoa powder
1 tsp. baking powder
1 tsp. salt

4 large eggs
1 tsp. vanilla extract

for the filling and glaze
1 cup chocolate ice cream
1/2 cup (3 1/2 oz.) semisweet chocolate chips
1/3 cup heavy cream

Preheat the oven to 350°F (175°C). Place 18 paper baking cups in muffin pans. Combine all the cupcake ingredients in a medium bowl and beat with an electric mixer until smooth and creamy, about 2 to 3 minutes.

Spoon the batter into the cups. Bake for 20 minutes. Remove pans from the oven and cool for 5 minutes. Then remove the cupcakes and cool on a rack. When cool, slice the cupcakes horizontally and spread a little softened ice cream on the bottom slice. Place the top back on the cupcake and freeze. Prepare the glaze by melting the chocolate in a double boiler, or a medium bowl over a pan of simmering water, stirring until completely melted. Remove from the heat. Add the cream and stir until well combined. Cool slightly and spoon over the cupcakes. Return to the freezer to set.

Freeze in an airtight container for up to 3 months.

Makes 1 1/2 dozen

white chocolate & strawberry cupcakes

see variations page 105

Simple yet sophisticated — and perfect for a summer picnic!

for the cupcakes
1 cup (2 sticks) sweet butter, softened
1 cup granulated sugar
2 cups cake flour
1 tsp. baking powder
1/2 tsp. salt
4 large eggs
1 tsp. strawberry extract
1/2 cup (3 1/2 oz.) white chocolate chips

for the frosting
1 cup cream cheese, softened
1 1/2 cups confectioners' sugar, sifted
1 tsp. vanilla extract
3 tbsp. sweet butter, softened
3 tbsp. chopped fresh strawberries

Preheat the oven to 350°F (175°C). Place 18 paper baking cups in muffin pans. Combine the butter, sugar, flour, baking powder, salt, eggs, and strawberry extract in a medium bowl. Beat with an electric mixer until light and creamy, about 2 to 3 minutes. Stir in the chocolate chips. Spoon the batter into the cups. Bake for 20 minutes. Remove pans from the oven and cool for 5 minutes. Then remove the cupcakes and cool on a rack. To make the frosting, beat the cream cheese, confectioners' sugar, vanilla, and butter until smooth and creamy. Stir in the chopped strawberries. Spread frosting on top of the cupcakes.

Store unfrosted in an airtight container for up to 2 days, or freeze for up to 3 months.

Makes 1 1/2 dozen

chocolate & chili cupcakes

see variations page 106

The Spanish conquistadors brought chocolate back from Mexico, a fact that inspired this delicious combination of semisweet chocolate and tingling chili.

for the cupcakes
1 cup (2 sticks) sweet butter, softened
1 cup granulated sugar
1 1/2 cups cake flour
4 tbsp. Dutch-process cocoa powder
1 tsp. baking powder
1/2 tsp. salt
4 large eggs

2 tsp. chipotle chili powder
1/2 cup (3 1/2 oz.) semisweet chocolate chips

for the frosting
1 1/2 cups confectioners' sugar, sifted
1/2 cup Dutch-process cocoa powder
3 tbsp. Tia Maria
1/2 cup (1 stick) sweet butter, softened

Preheat the oven to 350°F (175°C). Place 18 paper baking cups in muffin pans. Combine all the cupcake ingredients, except the chocolate chips, in a large bowl and beat with an electric mixer until smooth, about 2 to 3 minutes. Stir in the chocolate chips. Spoon the batter into the cups. Bake for 20 minutes. Remove pans from the oven and cool for 5 minutes. Then remove the cupcakes and cool on a rack.

To make the frosting, blend all the ingredients together in a food processor. Spread the frosting on the cooled cupcakes.

Store unfrosted in an airtight container for up to 2 days.

Makes 1 1/2 dozen

white chocolate &
macadamia nut cupcakes

see variations page 107

Technically, white chocolate is not a chocolate, but it tastes just as decadent!

for the cupcakes
1 cup (2 sticks) sweet butter, softened
1 cup granulated sugar
2 cups cake flour
1 tsp. baking powder
1/2 tsp. salt
4 large eggs
1 tsp. vanilla extract
1/2 cup (3 1/2 oz.) white chocolate chips

for the frosting
1 cup (7 oz.) white chocolate chips
5 tbsp. milk
1 1/2 cups confectioners' sugar, sifted
3 tbsp. chopped, toasted macadamia nuts

Preheat the oven to 350°F (175°C). Place 18 paper baking cups in muffin pans. Combine all the cupcake ingredients, except the chocolate chips, in a large bowl and beat with an electric mixer until smooth and pale, about 2 to 3 minutes. Stir in the chocolate chips. Spoon the batter into the cups. Bake for 20 minutes. Remove pans from the oven and cool for 5 minutes. Then remove the cupcakes and cool on a rack. To make the frosting, melt the chocolate and milk in a double boiler, stirring frequently. Remove from the heat and beat in the confectioners' sugar until smooth. Spread over the cupcakes and sprinkle with the nuts.

Store unfrosted in an airtight container for up to 2 days.

Makes 1 1/2 dozen

chocolate fudge-frosted cupcakes

see variations page 108

This fudge frosting is bound to bring even the mildest chocaholics to their knees!

for the cupcakes
1 cup (2 sticks) sweet butter, softened
1 cup granulated sugar
2 cups cake flour
1 tsp. baking powder
1/2 tsp. salt
4 large eggs
1 tsp. vanilla extract

for the frosting
3 1/2 oz. semisweet chocolate, roughly chopped
2 tbsp. milk
1/4 cup (1/2 stick) sweet butter
3/4 cup confectioners' sugar, sifted

Preheat the oven to 350°F (175°C). Place 18 paper baking cups into muffin pans. Combine all the cupcake ingredients in a medium bowl and beat with an electric mixer until smooth and pale, about 2 to 3 minutes. Spoon the batter into the cups. Bake for 20 minutes. Remove the pans from the oven and cool for 5 minutes. Remove the cupcakes and cool on the rack.

To make the frosting, gently heat the chocolate, milk, and butter in a small, heavy saucepan, stirring until melted. Remove from the heat and beat in the confectioners' sugar. Swirl the frosting onto the cooled cupcakes.

Store unfrosted in an airtight container for up to 3 days, or freeze for up to 3 months.

Makes 1 1/2 dozen

devil's food cupcakes

see variations page 109

These cupcakes are incredibly rich and moist delights!

for the cupcakes
2 cups cake flour
1 tsp. baking powder
1/2 tsp. salt
1 cup packed light brown sugar
1 cup (2 sticks) sweet butter, softened
2 large eggs, separated
3 1/2 oz. semisweet chocolate, melted
1 tsp. vanilla extract
1/2 cup milk

for the frosting
1/2 cup (1 stick) sweet butter, softened
1 tbsp. milk
3 1/2 oz. semisweet chocolate, melted
1 tsp. vanilla extract
3/4 cup confectioners' sugar, sifted

Preheat the oven to 350°F (175°C). Place 18 paper baking cups into muffin pans. Sift the flour, baking powder, and salt and set aside. In a medium bowl, cream the sugar and butter. Add the egg yolks and beat well. Add the melted chocolate and vanilla, mixing well. Add the flour and milk alternately, beating well with each addition. Beat the egg whites in a medium bowl until soft peaks form, and gently fold them into the batter. Spoon the batter into the cups. Bake for 20 minutes. Remove pans from the oven and cool for 5 minutes. Then remove the cupcakes and cool on a rack. To make the frosting, cream the butter in a medium bowl. Beat in the milk until smooth. Stir in the chocolate and vanilla. Beat in the confectioners' sugar until thick and creamy. Spread over the cupcakes.

Store unfrosted in an airtight container for up to 2 days, or freeze for up to 3 months.

Makes 1 1/2 dozen

chocolate & cherry cupcakes

see variations page 110

The classic German dessert "Black Forest Cake" was the inspiration for this cupcake.

for the cupcakes
1 1/2 cups cake flour
4 tbsp. Dutch-process cocoa powder
1 tsp. baking powder
1/2 tsp. salt
1 cup granulated sugar
1 cup (2 sticks) sweet butter, softened
4 large eggs

1/2 cup pitted and chopped sweet cherries
2 tbsp. kirsch (or other cherry-flavored liqueur)

for the topping
3/4 cup heavy cream
3 tbsp. confectioners' sugar, sifted
12 whole sweet cherries
3 1/2 oz. semisweet chocolate bar

Preheat the oven to 325°F (160°C). Place 18 paper baking cups in muffin pans. In a medium bowl, sift together the flour, cocoa, salt and baking powder. Set aside. Cream the sugar and butter in a large bowl until smooth. Add the eggs one at a time, beating well with each addition. Add the flour mixture and the cherries, and stir until well combined. Spoon the batter into the cups. Bake for 20 minutes. Remove pans from the oven and cool for 5 minutes. Pour a little kirsch over each cupcake. Remove the cupcakes from the pans and cool on a rack.

For the topping, whip the cream and confectioners' sugar together until slightly stiff. Using a vegetable peeler, shave curls of chocolate from the bar. Garnish the cupcakes with a dollop of cream. Place a cherry in the center and chocolate around it. Store unfrosted in an airtight container for up to 3 days.

Makes 1 1/2 dozen

mint chocolate cupcakes

see variations page 111

Mint is a versatile herb that complements both sweet and savory dishes.

for the cupcakes
1 1/2 cups cake flour
4 tbsp. Dutch-process cocoa powder
1 tsp. baking powder
1/2 tsp. salt
1 cup granulated sugar
1 cup (2 sticks) sweet butter, softened
4 large eggs
1 tsp. mint extract
1/2 cup (3 1/2 oz.) semisweet chocolate chips

for the frosting
1/3 cup (2/3 stick) sweet butter, softened
2 cups confectioners' sugar, sifted
1 tsp. mint extract
Green food coloring
1/2 cup (3 1/2 oz.) semisweet chocolate chips

Preheat the oven to 325°F (160°C). Place 18 paper baking cups into muffin pans. In a medium bowl, sift together the flour, cocoa, baking powder, and salt. Set aside. Beat the sugar and butter together in a large bowl until smooth. Add the eggs one at a time, beating well after each addition. Add the flour mixture gradually, stirring until well combined. Stir in the mint extract and chocolate chips. Spoon the mixture into the cups. Bake for 20 minutes. Remove the pans from the oven and cool for 5 minutes. Then remove the cupcakes and cool on a rack. To make the frosting, beat the butter and confectioners' sugar in a small bowl until smooth and creamy. Stir in the mint extract and just enough food coloring to turn the frosting a mint green. Frost the cupcakes and decorate with chocolate chips.

Store unfrosted in an airtight container for up to 3 days, or freeze for up to 3 months.

Makes 1 1/2 dozen

chocolate chip & raisin brioches

see variations page 112

You'll find yourself drawn to the breakfast table by the aroma of these sweet breads, a perfect accompaniment to steaming hot coffee.

1/2 tbsp. active dry yeast
1/2 cup warm water
1 tsp. sugar
2 1/2 cups all-purpose flour
4 large eggs
1/4 cup granulated sugar

Pinch of salt
1/2 cup (1 stick) sweet butter, softened
1/2 cup (3 1/2 oz.) raisins
1/2 cup (3 1/2 oz.) semisweet chocolate chips
1 beaten egg

Combine the yeast, water, and the teaspoon of sugar in a large bowl. Stir well and leave in a warm place for 10 minutes. Stir in 1/2 cup of the flour until the mixture becomes a smooth paste. Beat the eggs and add them to the yeast mixture. Add the sugar and salt. Stir in the remaining flour, and mix until the dough is soft and slightly sticky. Leave in a warm place, covered with plastic wrap, for 45 minutes or until doubled in bulk. Preheat the oven to 400°F (200°C). Grease 12 mini brioche or muffin molds. Beat the butter, raisins, and chocolate chips into the dough. Fill the molds halfway. Leave in a warm place to rise for about 20 minutes, until the dough has risen to fill about two-thirds of each mold.

Brush each brioche with a little of the beaten egg and bake for 20 minutes. Cool in the molds for 5 minutes, remove, and cool on a rack.

Store in an airtight container for up to 2 days.

Makes 1 dozen

chocolate hazelnut cupcakes

see variations page 113

A timeless combination . . . with very little flour in the mix!

1/2 cup (1 stick) sweet butter
1/2 cup (3 1/2 oz.) semisweet chocolate chips
1/2 cup granulated sugar

4 large eggs, separated
2 tbsp. all-purpose flour
1/2 cup (1 1/2 oz.) chopped, toasted hazelnuts

Preheat the oven to 325°F (160°C). Place 12 paper baking cups in a muffin pan. Melt the butter and chocolate in a double boiler, or medium bowl over a pan of simmering water, stirring until completely melted. Cool slightly.

Beat the sugar and egg yolks in a medium bowl until thick and creamy. Stir the butter and chocolate, flour, and hazelnuts into the egg mixture.

In a medium bowl, beat the egg whites to soft peaks, and gently fold into the chocolate mixture. Spoon the batter into the cups. Bake for 20 minutes. Remove pan from the oven and cool for 5 minutes. Then remove the cupcakes and cool on a rack.

Store refrigerated in an airtight container for up to 2 days, or freeze for up to 3 months.

Makes 1 dozen

chocolate orange cupcakes

see variations page 114

Orange extract helps sweeten the bitterness of the chocolate.

for the cupcakes
1 cup (2 sticks) sweet butter, softened
1 cup granulated sugar
2 cups cake flour
2 tsp. baking powder
1 tsp. salt
4 large eggs
1 tsp. orange extract

1 1/2 tbsp. grated orange zest
1/2 cup (3 1/2 oz.) semisweet chocolate chips

for the glaze
1/2 cup (3 1/2 oz.) semisweet chocolate chips
1/3 cup heavy cream
1 tsp. orange extract

Preheat the oven to 350°F (175°C). Place 18 paper baking cups into muffin pans. Combine all the cupcake ingredients, except the chocolate chips, in a large bowl and beat with an electric mixer until smooth and pale, about 2 to 3 minutes. Stir in the chocolate chips. Spoon the batter into the cups. Bake for 20 minutes. Remove pans from the oven and cool for 5 minutes. Then remove the cupcakes and cool on a rack.

For the chocolate glaze, melt the chocolate in a double boiler or medium bowl over a pan of simmering water, stirring until completely melted. Add the cream and orange extract, and stir until well combined. Cool slightly and pour over the cupcakes. Refrigerate until set.

Store unglazed in an airtight container for up to 2 days, or freeze for up to 3 months.

Makes 1 1/2 dozen

chocolate brownie cupcakes

see variations page 115

Try these warm from the oven, topped with a generous spoonful of vanilla-flavored whipped cream.

for the cupcakes
3/4 cup (4 1/2 oz.) semisweet chocolate chips
1/2 cup (1 stick) sweet butter
2 large eggs
1 1/2 cups granulated sugar
1 tsp. vanilla extract
1 cup all-purpose flour

for the topping
1 cup heavy cream
1 tsp. vanilla extract
3 tbsp. confectioners' sugar, sifted

Preheat the oven to 325°F (160°C). Place 12 paper baking cups in a muffin pan. Melt the chocolate and butter in a double boiler or medium bowl set over a pan of simmering water, stirring until melted. Set aside to cool. In a medium bowl, beat the eggs, sugar, and vanilla until pale and thick. Fold in the chocolate and then the flour, mixing until well combined.

Spoon batter into the cups. Bake for 25 minutes.

Remove pan from the oven and cool for 5 minutes. Then remove the cupcakes and cool on a rack. For the topping, beat the cream in a medium bowl until semi-stiff. Fold in the vanilla and confectioners' sugar. Place a dollop or two on each brownie.

Makes 1 dozen

variations

chocolate mud cupcakes

see base recipe page 83

raspberry mud cupcakes
Prepare the basic cupcake recipe. Stir in 1/2 cup (3 1/2 oz.) lightly crushed raspberries to the mixture after adding the melted chocolate.

white chocolate mud cupcakes
Prepare the basic cupcake recipe. Substitute 1 1/2 cups (10 1/2 oz.) white chocolate chips for the semisweet chocolate chips.

macadamia mud cupcakes
Prepare the basic cupcake recipe. Toast and chop 1/2 cup (3 1/2 oz.) macadamia nuts, and stir them in after adding the melted chocolate.

mocha mud cupcakes
Prepare the basic cupcake recipe. Stir in 2 teaspoons instant espresso powder to the mixture after adding the melted chocolate.

chocolate truffle mud cupcakes
Prepare the basic cupcake recipe, substituting finely chopped chocolate truffles for the chocolate chips.

chocolate ice cream cupcakes

see base recipe page 85

vanilla ice cream cupcakes
Prepare the basic cupcake recipe, substituting 1 cup (3 oz.) vanilla ice cream for the chocolate ice cream.

chocolate chip & mint ice cream cupcakes
Prepare the basic cupcake recipe, substituting 1 cup (3 oz.) mint chocolate chip ice cream for the chocolate ice cream.

coffee ice cream cupcakes
Prepare the basic cupcake recipe, substituting 1 cup (3 oz.) coffee ice cream for the chocolate ice cream.

variations

white chocolate & strawberry cupcakes

see base recipe page 87

chocolate, strawberry & black pepper cupcakes
Prepare the basic cupcake recipe, but replace the white chocolate chips with
semisweet chocolate chips. Stir in 1 teaspoon freshly ground black pepper.

balsamic vinegar & strawberry cupcakes
Prepare the basic cupcake recipe, substituting 2 teaspoons sweet balsamic
vinegar for the vanilla extract. Omit the white chocolate chips.

lemony white chocolate & strawberry cupcakes
Prepare the basic cupcake recipe, adding 1 teaspoon grated lemon zest to
the batter.

variations

chocolate & chili cupcakes

see base recipe page 88

white chocolate & chili cupcakes
Prepare the basic cupcake recipe, substituting white chocolate chips for the semisweet chocolate chips.

vodka-frosted chocolate & chili cupcakes
Prepare the basic cupcake recipe. For the frosting, substitute 3 tablespoons vodka for the Tia Maria.

orange liqueur-frosted chocolate & chili cupcakes
Prepare the basic cupcake recipe. For the frosting, substitute 3 tablespoons Grand Marnier or another orange liqueur for the Tia Maria.

mexican chocolate & chili cupcakes
Prepare the basic cupcake recipe, substituting finely chopped Mexican chocolate for the semisweet chocolate chips.

white chocolate & macadamia nut cupcakes

see base recipe page 91

white chocolate, apricot & macadamia nut cupcakes
Prepare the basic cupcake recipe, substituting 1/4 cup (2 oz.) finely chopped dried apricots for half the white chocolate chips.

white chocolate & almond cupcakes
Prepare the basic cupcake recipe, substituting 1/4 cup (2 oz.) chopped blanched almonds for half the white chocolate chips. For the frosting, substitute 3 tablespoons toasted almonds for the macadamia nuts.

white chocolate, cranberry & macadamia nut cupcakes
Prepare the basic cupcake recipe, using only 1/4 cup (2 oz.) white chocolate chips and adding 1/2 cup (3 1/2 oz.) dried cranberries and 1 tablespoon orange zest.

chocolate fudge-frosted cupcakes

see base recipe page 92

candy fudge-frosted cupcakes
Prepare the basic cupcake recipe. For the frosting, add 1/2 cup (3 1/2 oz.) lightly crushed chocolate candies to the mixture after creaming the other ingredients.

white chocolate fudge-frosted cupcakes
Prepare the basic cupcake recipe. For the frosting, substitute 1/2 cup (3 1/2 oz.) white chocolate for the semisweet chocolate, and add 1 teaspoon vanilla extract.

fudge-frosted raisin cupcakes
Prepare the basic cupcake recipe, and add 1/2 cup (3 1/2 oz.) golden raisins to the mixture after creaming the batter.

truffle-frosted cupcakes
Prepare the basic cupcake recipe. For the frosting, substitute chopped chocolate truffles for the semisweet chocolate.

devil's food cupcakes

see base recipe page 93

coffee-frosted devil's food cupcakes
Prepare the basic cupcake recipe. For the frosting, mix 1 teaspoon hot coffee
with 2 tablespoons coffee granules and stir until dissolved. Leave to cool.
Stir the cooled coffee into the chocolate frosting.

white chocolate-frosted devil's food cupcakes
Prepare the basic cupcake recipe. For the frosting, substitute 1/2 cup
(3 1/2 oz.) melted white chocolate for the semisweet chocolate.

hazelnut & chocolate-frosted devil's food cupcakes
Prepare the basic cupcake recipe. For the frosting, add 1/2 cup (3 1/2 oz.)
chopped toasted hazelnuts after combining the other ingredients.

sour cream devil's food cupcakes
Prepare the basic cupcake recipe, substituting 1/2 cup (4 oz.) sour cream for
1 stick of the butter.

red devil cupcakes
Prepare the basic cupcake recipe, adding 1 tablespoon red food coloring to
the batter.

chocolate & cherry cupcakes

see base recipe page 94

slivered almond & cherry cupcakes
Prepare the basic cupcake recipe, folding 3 tablespoons toasted slivered almonds to the cream after it has been whipped.

choc & prune cupcakes
Prepare the basic cupcake recipe, substituting 1/2 cup (3 1/2 oz.) chopped prunes for the cherries. For the frosting, substitute 3 tablespoons chopped prunes for the whole cherries.

choc & blueberry cupcakes
Prepare the basic cupcake recipe, substituting 1/2 cup (3 1/2 oz.) crushed blueberries for the cherries. For the frosting, substitute 3 tablespoons blueberries for the cherries.

choc & coffee cupcakes
Prepare the basic cupcake recipe, substituting Kahlua for kirsch. For the frosting, substitute 1 cup (6 oz.) chocolate-covered espresso beans for the sweet cherries.

mint chocolate cupcakes

see base recipe page 96

raisin & mint chocolate cupcakes
Prepare the basic cupcake recipe, adding 1/2 cup (3 1/2 oz.) golden raisins along with the chocolate chips.

orange & mint chocolate cupcakes
Prepare the basic cupcake recipe, substituting 1/2 cup (3 1/2 oz.) orange chocolate chunks for the semisweet chocolate chips.

peppermint chocolate cupcakes
Prepare the basic cupcake recipe, substituting peppermint extract for mint extract. In the frosting, omit the food coloring, substitute peppermint extract for mint extract, and use peppermint candies in place of semisweet chocolate chips.

chocolate mint geranium cupcakes
Prepare the basic cupcake recipe. For the frosting, substitute 1/2 cup (3 tbsp.) fresh chocolate mint geranium leaves for chocolate chips on top of the cupcakes.

variations

chocolate chip & raisin brioches

see base recipe page 98

saffron, chocolate chip, & raisin brioches
Prepare the basic brioche recipe, adding a pinch of saffron to the dry ingredients.

white chocolate & macadamia nut brioches
Prepare the basic brioche recipe, substituting 1/2 cup (3 1/2 oz.) white chocolate chips and 1/2 cup (3 1/2 oz.) chopped macadamia nuts for the chocolate chips and raisins.

chocolate & cinnamon brioches
Prepare the basic brioche recipe, adding 2 teaspoons cinnamon to the flour.

chocolate & dried cherry brioches
Prepare the basic brioche recipe, substituting dried cherries for raisins.

chocolate chip & banana brioches
Prepare the basic brioche recipe, substituting 1/2 cup mashed banana (about 1 banana) for raisins.

variations

chocolate hazelnut cupcakes

see base recipe page 99

chocolate hazelnut & cranberry cupcakes
Prepare the basic cupcake recipe, adding 3 tablespoons chopped dried cranberries to the egg mixture.

chocolate hazelnut & orange cupcakes
Prepare the basic cupcake recipe, adding 2 tablespoons finely grated orange zest to the egg mixture.

chocolate macadamia nut cupcakes
Prepare the basic cupcake recipe, substituting 1/2 cup (3 1/2 oz.) toasted and chopped macadamia nuts for the hazelnuts.

chocolate pecan cupcakes
Prepare the basic cupcake recipe, substituting 1/2 cup (3 1/2 oz.) toasted and chopped pecans for the hazelnuts.

chocolate almond cupcakes
Prepare the basic cupcake recipe, adding 1 teaspoon almond extract and substituting 1/2 cup (3 1/2 oz.) toasted flaked almonds for the hazelnuts.

variations

chocolate orange cupcakes

see base recipe page 100

chocolate orange marshmallow-centered cupcakes
Bake and cool the cupcakes. Slice the top off each cupcake and hollow out a small hole. Push 1 mini marshmallow into the hole. Place the "lid" back on and frost with the chocolate glaze.

chocolate orange & vanilla custard cupcakes
Bake and cool the cupcakes. Slice the top off each cupcake and hollow out a small hole. Pipe 1 teaspoon vanilla pie filling into the hole. Replace the "lid" and frost with the chocolate glaze.

white chocolate & vanilla cupcakes
Prepare the basic cupcake recipe, substituting white chocolate chips for the semisweet chocolate chips and vanilla extract for the orange extract. Omit the orange zest. Use white chocolate chips for the glaze instead of semisweet chocolate.

chocolate candied orange-centered cupcakes
Bake and cool the cupcakes. Slice the top off each cupcake and hollow out a small hole. Push 1 small piece candied orange slice into the hole. Place the "lid" back on and frost with the chocolate glaze.

chocolate brownie cupcakes

see base recipe page 102

pecan brownie cupcakes
Prepare the basic cupcake recipe. Stir 1/2 cup (3 1/2 oz.) chopped pecans into the mixture with the chocolate chips.

dalmatian brownie cupcakes
Prepare the basic cupcake recipe, substituting white chocolate chips for half the quantity of semisweet chocolate chips.

chocolate fudge-frosted brownie cupcakes
Prepare the basic cupcake recipe, and omit the topping. To make the frosting, combine 1/2 cup (3 1/2 oz.) semisweet chocolate, 2 tablespoons milk, and 4 tablespoons sweet butter in a medium saucepan and stir until the chocolate has melted. Cool slightly and add 3 tablespoons confectioners' sugar. Mix until smooth.

chocolate brownie cupcake sundae
Prepare the basic cupcake recipe. To serve, place a cupcake on each plate. Top with a scoop of ice cream, a drizzle of hot fudge or caramel sauce, and a dollop of the vanilla cream topping.

decadent cupcakes

The recipes in this chapter will leave no doubt in your mind that the cupcake is most definitely a grown-up treat. From baked cheesecakes to brioche bread pudding to Florentine cupcakes, this chapter provides luxurious desserts in individual-size portions!

florentine cupcakes

see variations page 136

Savor *la dolce vita* when you bite into these Italian-inspired cupcakes.

for the cupcakes
1 cup (2 sticks) sweet butter, softened
1 cup granulated sugar
2 cups cake flour
2 tsp. baking powder
1 tsp. salt
4 large eggs
1/2 cup buttermilk
1 tsp. vanilla extract

for the topping
3 tbsp. slivered almonds
3 tbsp. Corn Flakes
1/2 cup (3 1/2 oz.) roughly chopped candied
    cherries
3 tbsp. golden raisins
5 tbsp. condensed milk
2 oz. semisweet chocolate, melted
2 oz. white chocolate, melted

Preheat the oven to 350°F (175°C). Place 18 paper baking cups in muffin pans. Combine all the cupcake ingredients in a large bowl and beat with an electric mixer until smooth and pale, about 2 to 3 minutes. Spoon the batter into the cups. Bake for 20 minutes. Remove pans from the oven and cool for 5 minutes. Then remove the cupcakes and cool on a rack.

For the florentine topping, combine all the ingredients except the chocolate in a small bowl. Spoon small teaspoons of the mixture onto silicone-lined cookie sheets. Bake for 5 minutes, until golden. Remove from the oven and cool for 1 minute. Remove the florentines from the sheet and crumble. Scatter over the cooled cupcakes and drizzle with the chocolate.

Store in an airtight container for up to 2 days, or freeze for up to 3 months.

Makes 1 1/2 dozen

strawberries & cream cupcakes

see variations page 137

This recipe is great for lazy summer days when plump, sweet, and juicy strawberries are at the height of their season.

for the cupcakes
1 cup (2 sticks) sweet butter, softened
1 cup granulated sugar
2 cups cake flour
2 tsp. baking powder
1 tsp. salt
4 large eggs
1/2 cup buttermilk
1 tsp. vanilla extract

for the topping
1 cup heavy cream
4 tbsp. confectioners' sugar, sifted
1 tsp. vanilla extract
4 cups sliced small strawberries
4 tbsp. strawberry jelly
1 tbsp. water

Preheat the oven to 350°F (175°C). Place 18 paper baking cups in muffin pans. Combine all the cupcake ingredients in a medium bowl and beat with an electric mixer until smooth and pale, about 2 to 3 minutes. Spoon the batter into the cups. Bake for 20 minutes. Remove pans from the oven and cool for 5 minutes. Then remove the cupcakes and cool on a rack.

For the topping, beat the cream, confectioners' sugar, and vanilla in a small bowl until soft peaks form. Spoon onto the cupcakes and arrange the strawberries on top. In a small saucepan heat the jelly and water until melted. Brush the mixture on top of the strawberries. Chill until ready to serve.

Store, without topping, in an airtight container in the refrigerator for up to 2 days.

Makes 1 1/2 dozen

baked cheesecakes

see variations page 138

These mouthwatering little cupcakes make stunning individual desserts. Make them ahead of time and all you'll have to do is pop them on a plate when your guests are ready.

1 cup (4 1/2 oz.) graham cracker crumbs
5 tbsp. sweet butter, melted
2 cups ricotta cheese
2 cups cream cheese, softened

2 tsp. vanilla extract
1 1/2 cups confectioners' sugar, sifted
3 large eggs
1 1/2 cups fresh blueberries

Preheat the oven to 325°F (160°C). Place 12 paper baking cups in a muffin pan.

Put the cracker crumbs into a medium bowl and stir in the butter. Spoon tablespoons of the crumb mixture into the cups, pressing firmly into the bottom. Chill until set.

In a large bowl, beat the ricotta until smooth. Add the cream cheese, vanilla, and confectioners' sugar, blending until smooth. Slowly add the eggs, blending well. Spoon the mixture into the cups.

Bake for 25 minutes. Remove pan from oven and cool for 5 minutes. Then remove the cupcakes and cool on a rack. Chill until time to serve. Serve topped with blueberries.

Store covered for up to 2 days in the refrigerator.

Makes 1 dozen

kahlua & orange cupcakes

see variations page 139

The combination of Kahlua and orange is wonderful. It makes a delightful drink, and a scrumptious cupcake, too!

for the cupcakes
1 cup (2 sticks) sweet butter, softened
1 cup granulated sugar
2 cups cake flour
2 tsp. baking powder
1 tsp. salt
4 large eggs
1/2 cup buttermilk
1 tsp. orange extract

for the frosting
2 cups confectioners' sugar, sifted
1/2 cup (1 stick) sweet butter, softened
1/4 cup sour cream
2 tbsp. Kahlua
1 tbsp. grated orange zest

Preheat the oven to 350°F (175°C). Place 18 paper baking cups in muffin pans. Combine all the cupcake ingredients in a medium bowl and beat with an electric mixer until smooth and pale, about 2 to 3 minutes. Spoon the batter into the cups. Bake for 20 minutes. Remove pans from the oven and cool for 5 minutes. Then remove the cupcakes and cool on a rack.

To make the frosting, beat the confectioners' sugar and butter in a small bowl until soft and creamy. Beat in the sour cream, Kahlua, and orange zest. Swirl onto the cooled cupcakes.

Store unfrosted in an airtight container for up to 2 days, or freeze for up to 3 months.

Makes 1 1/2 dozen

hot chocolate fondant cupcakes

see variations page 140

These cupcakes are very simple but must be served immediately. You can prepare the ramekins and batter in advance.

for the cupcakes
1 1/2 cups (7 1/2 oz.) bittersweet chocolate,
    broken into pieces
1 cup (2 sticks) sweet butter, softened
4 large eggs
4 large egg yolks
1/2 cup granulated sugar
3 tbsp. all-purpose flour

for the topping
1 cup sour cream or crème fraiche
Cocoa powder or confectioners' sugar
    for dusting

Preheat the oven to 375°F (190°C). Butter 8 medium-sized ramekins. Dust each with flour, and tap out the excess. Melt the chocolate and butter in a double boiler or medium bowl over a pan of simmering water. Stir until smooth. Set aside to cool. In a large bowl, beat the eggs, egg yolks, and sugar until pale and creamy. Gradually add the melted chocolate, stirring until combined. Stir in the flour. Pour the batter into the prepared ramekins and bake for 15 minutes, or until the tops are set.

Turn out onto serving plates. Top each with a dollop of sour cream, and dust with cocoa powder or confectioners' sugar. Serve swiftly.

Makes 8

brioche bread pudding cupcakes

see variations page 141

Try this rich and robust cupcake recipe for an unusual and tasty twist on the classic bread pudding.

for the custard
2 large eggs
1/2 cup granulated sugar
1 tsp. vanilla extract
2 cups heavy cream

for the cupcakes
12 thin slices brioche (crusts removed)
4 tbsp. sweet butter
3/4 cup fresh raspberries

To make the custard, cream the eggs, sugar, and vanilla in a small bowl. Add the cream, stir well, and put aside.

Preheat the oven to 350°F (175°C). Grease 12 small molds with a little melted butter. Butter both sides of the bread and cut each slice into 12 small triangles. Push 3 triangles of bread into each mold, covering the bottom. Add a layer of raspberries. Pour a layer of custard over the raspberries. Repeat the process until there are four layers of each in each mold.

Place the molds in a roasting pan. Pour boiling water into the pan until it reaches halfway up the molds. Bake until golden and firm, about 25 minutes. If the puddings begin to color too much, cover the pan with aluminum foil.

Turn the puddings out of the cups and serve warm.

Makes 1 dozen

mini espresso cupcakes

see variations page 142

Making these cupcakes in espresso cups adds a special touch to the end of a meal.

for the cupcakes
1 1/2 cups all-purpose flour
1 1/2 tsp. baking powder
Pinch of salt
1/2 cup malted milk powder
1/4 cup dark espresso coffee
1 cup granulated sugar
2 eggs
1/2 cup (1 stick) sweet butter, softened

for the frosting
1 cup (2 sticks) sweet butter, softened
3 cups confectioners' sugar, sifted
1 tbsp. instant coffee granules
2 tsp. hot coffee
1 tsp. vanilla extract

Preheat the oven to 350°F (175°C). Lightly grease 18 espresso cups (or use muffin papers in a muffin pan). Sift the flour, baking powder, and salt into a medium bowl. Combine the milk powder and coffee in a small bowl. Beat the sugar, eggs, and butter in a medium bowl until light and creamy. Add the flour and coffee mixtures alternately to the egg mixture. Spoon the mixture into the cups. Bake for 15 minutes. Remove cups from oven and cool on a rack.

To make the frosting, beat the butter and confectioners' sugar in a bowl until soft and creamy. Add the coffee granules to the hot coffee and stir. Beat into the butter and sugar mixture, and then stir in the vanilla. Dollop frosting on cooled cupcakes in the espresso cups.

Store unfrosted for up to 2 days in an airtight container, or freeze for up to 3 months.

Makes 1 1/2 dozen

almond & raspberry friands

see variations page 143

Try using different oval or rectangular-shaped friand pans. They are available from specialty cookware stores. If you can't find a friand pan, a regular muffin pan works fine.

1 3/4 cups (2 sticks plus 3 tbsp.) sweet butter, softened
1 cup (3 1/2 oz.) ground almonds
6 large egg whites

2/3 cup all-purpose flour
1/2 cup fresh raspberries
1/2 cup granulated sugar
Confectioners' sugar for dusting

Preheat the oven to 350°F (175°C). Grease 12 small friand pans with a little of the butter. Mix all the ingredients in a large bowl, reserving half the raspberries, until just combined.

Pour the batter into the prepared pans and scatter the remaining raspberries on top. Bake for 25 minutes, until golden and firm.

Remove pans from the oven and cool for 5 minutes. Turn friands out onto a rack and cool completely. Serve dusted with confectioners' sugar.

Store in an airtight container for up to 2 days.

Makes 1 dozen

key lime cupcakes

see variations page 144

An unusual take on the classic key lime pie. The cupcakes look great and taste even better!

for the cupcakes
1 cup (2 sticks) sweet butter, softened
1 cup granulated sugar
2 cups cake flour
2 tsp. baking powder
1 tsp. salt
4 large eggs
1/2 cup buttermilk
1 tsp. vanilla extract

for the filling
1/3 cup key lime juice
1 (14-oz.) can condensed milk

for the meringue
3 egg whites
1/4 tsp. cream of tartar
1/3 cup granulated sugar

Preheat the oven to 350°F (175°C). Place 18 paper baking cups in muffin pans. Place all the cupcake ingredients in a large bowl, and beat with an electric mixer until smooth and pale, about 2 to 3 minutes. Spoon the batter into the cups. Bake for 20 minutes. Remove pans from the oven and cool for 5 minutes. Then remove the cupcakes and cool on a rack.

For the filling, combine the lime juice and condensed milk in a small bowl. Remove the top from each cupcake and hollow out a small hole. Spoon the filling into the hole and replace the top. For the meringue, beat the egg whites and cream of tartar until soft peaks form. Add one-third of the sugar and beat for 1 minute. Repeat until all the sugar has been added. Increase the oven temperature to 450°F (230°C). Spoon or pipe the meringue on top of the cupcakes. Bake for 5 minutes until golden. Store for no more than 1 day in an airtight container.

Makes 1 1/2 dozen

pineapple upside-down cupcakes

see variations page 145

A classic cake scaled down to a cupcake! When turning out the cupcakes, allow the sweet juices of the pineapple to be absorbed into the golden sponge.

for the topping
1/2 cup (1 stick) sweet butter, melted
1 (20-oz.) can crushed pineapple
3/4 cup packed brown sugar

for the cupcakes
1 cup (2 sticks) sweet butter, softened
1 cup granulated sugar

2 cups cake flour
2 tsp. baking powder
1 tsp. salt
4 large eggs
1/2 cup buttermilk
1 tsp. vanilla extract

Preheat the oven to 350°F (175°C). Grease two 12-cup muffin pans with butter, and dust with a little flour, tapping out the excess. In the bottom of each cup, drizzle 1 tablespoon melted butter, 1 tablespoon pineapple, and 1 tablespoon brown sugar.

Place all the cupcake ingredients in a large bowl and beat with an electric mixer until smooth and pale, about 2 to 3 minutes. Spoon the batter on top of the pineapple mixture in each cup. Bake for 25 minutes. Remove pans from the oven and cool for 10 minutes.

Turn out the cupcakes onto dessert plates, and serve warm with heavy cream if desired.

Store in an airtight container for up to 2 days.

Makes 2 dozen

little caramel cupcakes

see variations page 146

These delightful cupcakes contain a rich and gooey caramel surprise. They are an ideal companion for a cup of Earl Grey tea.

1/2 cup (1 stick) sweet butter, softened
3/4 cup packed brown sugar
2 large eggs, lightly beaten
2 tbsp. instant coffee granules
1 tbsp. boiling water

2 2/3 cups cake flour
2 tsp. baking powder
1 tsp. salt
1/2 cup milk
1/2 cup (3 1/2 oz.) soft caramels

Preheat the oven to 350°F (175°C). Place 12 paper baking cups in a muffin pan.

In a medium bowl, beat the butter and sugar until pale and creamy. Add the eggs slowly. In a small bowl, dissolve the coffee in the water. Beat the coffee into the butter mixture. Add the flour, baking powder, salt, and milk, and beat until well combined.

Spoon the mixture into the cups. Push a couple of the caramels into the center of each cupcake, and place them in the oven.

Bake for 20 minutes. Cool for 5 minutes in the pan. Turn onto a plate and serve while warm.

Makes 1 dozen

sticky toffee pudding cupcakes

see variations page 147

This is an old classic British pudding that has recently enjoyed a bit of a renaissance.

for the cupcakes
1 1/2 cups cake flour
1 1/2 tsp. baking powder
1/2 tsp. salt
2/3 cup packed brown sugar
1/2 cup milk
1 large egg
1 tsp. vanilla extract

3 tbsp. sweet butter, melted
1 1/4 cups (7 oz.) chopped dates

for the topping
1/2 cup packed brown sugar
4 tbsp. sweet butter
2/3 cup boiling water

Preheat the oven to 375°F (190°C). Line 8 muffin pans with baking parchment. In a medium bowl, combine the flour, baking powder, salt, and sugar. In a separate medium bowl, beat the milk, egg, vanilla, and butter until smooth and pale, about 2 to 3 minutes. Pour the batter over the flour mixture and stir with a wooden spoon. Fold in the dates. Scrape the mixture into the muffin pans, filling each cup about halfway. For the topping, sprinkle 1 tablespoon of the sugar on top of the batter in each cup. Put a half-tablespoon piece of butter on top of each cupcake, then pour about 1 tablespoon water over each.

Bake for 25 minutes. Remove from oven and cool for 5 minutes in the pan. Invert onto plates, peel off the parchment, and serve immediately.

Makes 8

florentine cupcakes

see base recipe page 117

chocolate chip florentine cupcakes
Prepare the basic cupcake recipe, adding 1/2 cup (3 1/2 oz.) semisweet chocolate chips after creaming the batter.

cherry florentine cupcakes
Prepare the basic cupcake recipe, adding 3 tablespoons chopped candied cherries after creaming the batter.

almond florentine cupcakes
Prepare the basic cupcake recipe, adding 3 tablespoons chopped blanched almonds after creaming the batter.

tipsy florentine cupcakes
Prepare the basic cupcake recipe, substituting 1/4 cup (2 fl. oz.) Amaretto for 1/4 cup (2 fl. oz.) of the buttermilk.

variations

strawberries & cream cupcakes

see base recipe page 118

strawberries & white chocolate cupcakes
Prepare the basic cupcake recipe, adding 1/2 cup (3 1/2 oz.) chopped white chocolate chips to the creamed batter.

strawberries & honey cupcakes
Prepare the basic cupcake recipe. For the topping, substitute 2 tablespoons honey for the confectioners' sugar.

strawberries & lime cupcakes
Prepare the basic cupcake recipe. For the topping, substitute 1 tablespoon lime juice for the vanilla extract. Substitute 4 tablespoons lime jelly for the strawberry jelly.

berries & cream cupcakes
Prepare the basic cupcake recipe. For the topping, substitute 4 cups (1 lb.) mixed berries for the strawberries.

variations

baked cheesecakes

see base recipe page 120

banana & raisin baked cheesecakes
Prepare the basic cupcake recipe, adding 1/2 cup mashed banana (about 1 banana) to the cheese mixture before adding the eggs. Add 4 tablespoons raisins to the mixture after adding the egg.

raspberry baked cheesecakes
Prepare the basic cupcake recipe, adding 1/2 cup (3 oz.) fresh raspberries after mixing in the eggs.

maple syrup baked cheesecakes
Prepare the basic cupcake recipe, substituting 1/4 cup (2 fl. oz.) maple syrup for the confectioners' sugar.

almond baked cheesecakes
Prepare the basic cupcake recipe, substituting 1 teaspoon almond extract for 2 teaspoons vanilla.

kahlua & orange cupcakes

see base recipe page 122

white chocolate chip kahlua cupcakes
Prepare the basic cupcake recipe, adding 1/2 cup (3 1/2 oz.) white chocolate chips to the creamed batter.

raisin & brazil nut kahlua cupcakes
Prepare the basic cupcake recipe, adding 1/4 cup (2 oz.) raisins and 1/4 cup (2 oz.) chopped Brazil nuts to the creamed batter.

cointreau & orange cupcakes
Prepare the basic cupcake recipe, substituting Cointreau for Kahlua in the frosting.

variations

hot chocolate fondant cupcakes

see base recipe page 123

strawberry cream fondant cupcakes
Prepare the basic cupcake recipe. Purée 5 medium-size, fresh strawberries in a food processor. Beat 1 cup (8 fl. oz.) heavy cream with 1 teaspoon vanilla extract until it is soft but holds its shape. Fold in the puréed strawberries. Spoon over the hot cupcakes. Omit the basic topping.

orange cream fondant cupcakes
Prepare the basic cupcake recipe. Beat 1 cup (8 fl. oz.) heavy cream with 1 teaspoon orange extract and 2 tablespoons confectioners' sugar until it is soft but holds its shape. Spoon liberally over the hot cupcakes. Omit the basic topping.

crème chantilly fondant cupcakes
Prepare the basic cupcake recipe. Beat 1 cup (8 fl. oz.) heavy cream with 1 teaspoon vanilla extract and 2 tablespoons confectioners' sugar until it is soft but holds its shape. Spoon over the hot cupcakes. Omit the basic topping.

cappuccino fondant cupcakes
Prepare the basic cupcake recipe, adding 1 teaspoon cinnamon to the batter. Beat 1 cup (8 fl. oz.) heavy cream with 1 teaspoon coffee extract and 2 tablespoons confectioners' sugar until it is soft but holds its shape. Spoon liberally over the hot cupcakes. Omit the basic topping.

brioche bread pudding cupcakes

see base recipe page 125

blueberry bread pudding cupcakes
Prepare the basic cupcake recipe, substituting 3/4 cup (4 oz.) fresh blueberries for the raspberries.

cherry bread pudding cupcakes
Prepare the basic cupcake recipe, substituting 3/4 cup (5 oz.) chopped candied cherries for the raspberries.

chocolate chip bread pudding cupcakes
Prepare the basic cupcake recipe, substituting 3/4 cup (5 oz.) semisweet chocolate chips for the raspberries.

berry delicious bread pudding cupcakes
Prepare the basic cupcake recipe, substituting 1/4 cup (1 1/2 oz.) each of raspberries, blueberries, and sliced strawberries for the raspberries.

variations

mini espresso cupcakes

see base recipe page 126

mini chocolate espresso cupcakes
Prepare the basic cupcake recipe, adding 3 tablespoons chocolate chips after creaming the batter.

mini cinnamon espresso cupcakes
Prepare the basic cupcake recipe, sifting 2 teaspoons cinnamon into the dry ingredients.

mini espresso cupcakes with tia maria
Prepare the basic cupcake recipe, adding 2 tablespoons Tia Maria liqueur to the frosting.

mini caramel macchiatto cupcakes
Prepare the basic cupcake recipe. When the cupcakes have cooled, use a sharp knife to slice off the tops. Using a teaspoon, hollow out a small hole in the top of each cupcake. Spoon 1 teaspoon prepared caramel sauce into the small hole. Place the top back on the cupcake and frost.

almond & raspberry friands

see base recipe page 129

strawberry friands
Prepare the basic cupcake recipe, substituting 1/2 cup (3 1/2 oz.) fresh strawberries for the raspberries.

chocolate & pecan friands
Prepare the basic cupcake recipe, substituting 3 tablespoons chopped pecans and 3 tablespoons semisweet chocolate chips for the raspberries.

raisin friands
Prepare the basic cupcake recipe, substituting 1/2 cup (3 1/2 oz.) raisins for the raspberries.

almond & pear friands
Prepare the basic cupcake recipe, substituting 1/2 cup (3 oz.) peeled and chopped pears for the raspberries.

variations

key lime cupcakes

see base recipe page 131

ice cream meringue cupcakes
Prepare the basic cupcake recipe, substituting 1 teaspoon ice cream for the original filling in each cupcake. Pop the cupcakes into the freezer until ready to serve.

chocolate meringue cupcakes
Prepare the basic cupcake recipe. For the filling, substitute 1/2 cup (3 1/2 oz.) semisweet chocolate chips for the milk and lime juice. Melt the chocolate in a double boiler and cool slightly. Spoon the chocolate into the hole and refrigerate until set. Decorate with the meringue when the chocolate has cooled. Bake for 5 minutes until meringue is golden.

lemon meringue cupcakes
Prepare the basic cupcake recipe. For the filling, substitute 1/3 cup (3 fl. oz.) lemon juice for the key lime juice.

mango cupcakes
Prepare the basic cupcake recipe. For the filling, substitute 1/3 cup (3 fl. oz.) mango nectar for the key lime juice.

variations

pineapple upside-down cupcakes

see base recipe page 132

cherry pineapple upside-down cupcakes
Prepare the basic cupcake recipe. Add 1/2 cup (3 1/2 oz.) chopped cherries to
the pineapple mixture.

almond pineapple upside-down cupcakes
Prepare the basic cupcake recipe, adding 3 tablespoons chopped blanched
almonds to the cupcake batter.

orange pineapple upside-down cupcakes
Prepare the basic cupcake recipe, adding 2 teaspoons orange extract to the
cupcake batter.

pineapple coconut upside-down cupcakes
Prepare the basic cupcake recipe, adding 1/2 cup (2 1/2 oz.) sweetened,
flaked coconut to the cupcake batter.

apple brandy upside-down cupcakes
Prepare the basic cupcake recipe. Replace the pineapple mixture with 20 oz.
apples, peeled, cored, and sliced, 1/2 cup (1 stick) sweet butter, melted,
3/4 cup (7 oz.) packed brown sugar, and 4 tablespoons apple brandy.
Combine, and proceed as in base recipe.

variations

little caramel cupcakes

see base recipe page 134

chocolate chip & caramel cupcakes
Prepare the basic cupcake recipe, mixing 4 tablespoons semisweet chocolate chips into the batter after the milk has been added.

ginger & caramel cupcakes
Prepare the basic cupcake recipe, mixing 3 tablespoons chopped candied ginger into the batter after the milk has been added.

chocolate nougat cupcakes
Prepare the basic cupcake recipe, substituting 6 1/2 mini Baby Ruth bars for the caramel.

peanut butter cup cupcakes
Prepare the basic cupcake recipe, substituting 3 1/2 ounces of chopped chocolate-covered peanut butter cups for the caramel.

sticky toffee pudding cupcakes

see base recipe page 135

date & apricot pudding cupcakes
Prepare the basic cupcake recipe. Substitute 2/3 cup (4 oz.) dried apricots for half the chopped dates.

date & walnut pudding cupcakes
Prepare the basic cupcake recipe. Substitute 2/3 cup (4 oz.) chopped walnuts for half the chopped dates.

date & pistachio pudding cupcakes
Prepare the basic cupcake recipe. Substitute 2/3 cup (4 oz.) chopped pistachios for half the chopped dates.

sticky figgy pudding cupcakes
Prepare the basic cupcake recipe. Substitute 2/3 cup (4 oz.) chopped dried figs for half the chopped dates.

celebration
cupcakes

This chapter will provide inspiration for your next

special occasion, whether a holiday like Valentine's

Day, or a birthday or wedding.

easter egg nests

see variations page 164

These cute nests make the perfect gift for your little Easter bunnies.

for the cupcakes
1 cup (2 sticks) sweet butter, softened
1 cup granulated sugar
2 cups cake flour
2 tsp. baking powder
1 tsp. salt
4 large eggs
1/2 cup buttermilk
1 tsp. vanilla extract

for the frosting
3/4 cup (4 1/2 oz.) semisweet chocolate, chopped
2 tbsp. heavy cream
10 oz. chocolate, flaked
54 candy-covered mini chocolate eggs

Preheat the oven to 350°F (175°C). Place 18 paper baking cups in muffin pans. Combine all the cupcake ingredients in a large bowl and beat with an electric mixer until smooth and pale, about 2 to 3 minutes. Spoon the batter into the cups. Bake for 20 minutes. Remove pans from the oven and cool for 5 minutes. Then remove the cupcakes and cool on a rack.

To make the frosting, put the semisweet chocolate and cream in a small saucepan over a low heat. Stir gently until combined. Remove from the heat and stir until the mixture is smooth. Swirl onto the cooled cupcakes. Top with flaked chocolate and place 3 mini eggs on top of each one.

Store unfrosted in an airtight container for up to 3 days, or freeze for up to 3 months.

Makes 1 1/2 dozen

wedding cupcakes

see variations page 165

These cupcakes are perfect for a home-style wedding. Each of your guests can take one home as a memento of the day.

for the cupcakes
1 cup (2 sticks) sweet butter, softened
1 cup granulated sugar
2 cups cake flour
2 tsp. baking powder
1 tsp. salt
4 large eggs
1/2 cup buttermilk
1 tsp. vanilla extract

for the frosting
2 1/2 cups confectioners' sugar
2 tbsp. lemon juice
54 Jordan almonds
18 frosted roses

Preheat the oven to 350°F (175°C). Place 18 paper baking cups in muffin pans. Combine all the cupcake ingredients in a large bowl and beat with an electric mixer until smooth and pale, about 2 to 3 minutes.

Spoon the batter into the cups. Bake for 20 minutes. Remove pans from the oven and cool for 5 minutes. Then remove the cupcakes and cool on a rack.

To make the frosting, sift the confectioners' sugar into a medium bowl. Add the lemon juice gradually, until it holds its shape. Spread onto the cupcakes, and top with almonds and roses.

Store unfrosted in an airtight container for up to 3 days, or freeze for up to 3 months.

Makes 1 1/2 dozen

passover cupcakes

see variations page 166

Make these with matzoh meal, also known as cake meal. We have added fresh blueberries to these passover treats.

1 cup granulated sugar
1/2 cup vegetable oil
3 large eggs
1/2 cup matzoh meal

2 tbsp. potato starch
1 tsp. cinnamon
1 3/4 cups blueberries

Preheat the oven to 350°F (175°C). Place 12 paper baking cups in a muffin pan.

In a medium bowl, beat the sugar, oil, and eggs with an electric mixer for 2 to 3 minutes. Set aside. In a small bowl, sift together the matzoh meal, potato starch, and cinnamon. Add the dry ingredients to the egg mixture. Stir in the blueberries. Spoon the mixture into the cups.

Bake for 20 minutes. Remove pan from the oven and cool for 5 minutes. Then remove the cupcakes and cool on a rack.

Store in an airtight container for up to 3 days, or freeze for up to 3 months.

Makes 1 dozen

irish barm brack cupcakes

see variations page 167

Traditionally, a quarter and a ring are hidden in barm brack cakes. The person who finds the ring will soon be married and the person who finds the quarter will soon be wealthy.

1/2 cup (3 1/2 oz.) raisins
1/2 cup (3 1/2 oz.) golden raisins
1/2 cup (3 1/2 oz.) currants
1 cup brewed black tea
4 cups all-purpose flour
1 tsp. allspice

1/3 cup packed brown sugar
1 tsp. baking powder
Pinch of salt
1 large egg
1/2 cup (1 stick) sweet butter, melted

In a large bowl, soak the dried fruits in the tea. Leave overnight or for a minimum of 6 hours.

Preheat the oven to 400°F (200°C). Grease a 12-cup muffin pan with a little oil.

Mix the dry ingredients in a large bowl. In a separate large bowl, mix the egg and butter. Add the soaked and strained fruit, and stir well. Fold in the flour mixture.

Spoon the mixture into the prepared pan. (Optional: Place a ring in one of the cakes, and a quarter in another.) Bake for approximately 30 minutes until the cupcakes are a dark golden color. Remove pan from the oven and cool for 5 minutes. Then remove the cupcakes and cool on a rack. Serve with sweet butter.

Store in an airtight container for up to 5 days, or freeze for up to 3 months.

Makes 1 dozen

king cupcakes

see variations page 168

Our version of the classic Mardi Gras "king cake." The colors traditionally used on the cake represent justice, faith, and power.

for the cupcakes
1 cup (2 sticks) sweet butter, softened
1 cup granulated sugar
2 cups cake flour
2 tsp. baking powder
1 tsp. salt
4 large eggs
1/2 cup buttermilk
1 tsp. vanilla extract

for the frosting
2 1/2 cups confectioners' sugar
2 tbsp. lemon juice
2 tbsp. gold-colored sugar
2 tbsp. green-colored sugar
2 tbsp. purple-colored sugar

Preheat the oven to 350°F (175°C). Place 18 paper baking cups in muffin pans. Combine all the cupcake ingredients in a large bowl and beat with an electric mixer until smooth and pale, about 2 to 3 minutes. Spoon the batter into the cups. Bake for 20 minutes. Remove pans from the oven and cool for 5 minutes. Then remove the cupcakes and cool on a rack.

To make the frosting, sift the confectioners' sugar in a medium bowl. Slowly add the lemon juice until the mixture becomes firm but spreadable. Spread onto the cupcakes, and sprinkle with the colored sugar.

Store unfrosted in an airtight container for up to 3 days, or freeze for up to 3 months.

Makes 1 1/2 dozen

christmas tree cupcakes

see variations page 169

These fun and festive little cakes will look superb on your Christmas dessert table. You can find ready-to-roll fondant frosting at cake decorating and baking supply shops.

for the cupcakes
1 cup (2 sticks) sweet butter, softened
1 cup granulated sugar
2 cups cake flour
2 tsp. baking powder
1 tsp. salt
4 large eggs

1/2 cup buttermilk
1 tsp. vanilla extract

for the frosting
4 oz. ready-to-roll white fondant frosting
Green food coloring
2 tbsp. raspberry jam
Colored candy balls

Preheat the oven to 350°F (175°C). Place 18 paper baking cups in muffin pans. Combine all the cupcake ingredients into a large bowl and beat with an electric mixer until smooth and pale, about 2 to 3 minutes. Spoon the batter into the cups. Bake for 20 minutes. Remove pans from the oven and cool for 5 minutes. Then remove the cupcakes and cool on a rack. Dust 2 cookie sheets with confectioners' sugar. To make the frosting, divide the fondant in half. In a bowl, work green food coloring into one half and set aside. Roll the white fondant frosting to 1/8 in. (3 mm) thick. Cut 18 circles using a 2-inch (5-cm) cookie cutter and set them on one of the cookie sheets. Roll the green fondant frosting to 1/8 in. (3 mm) thick. Using a small Christmas tree cookie cutter, cut shapes out of the frosting and place them on the other cookie sheet to firm a little. Brush each cupcake with a little raspberry jam, then place a white fondant disc on top. Top with a Christmas tree and decorate with the colored balls.

Makes 1 1/2 dozen

snowflake cupcakes

see variations page 170

These cupcakes are delightful for a Christmas gathering. You can serve them on Christmas Eve when Santa's sleigh has set off and the kids are tucked into bed.

for the cupcakes
1 cup (2 sticks) sweet butter, softened
1 cup granulated sugar
2 cups cake flour
2 tsp. baking powder
1 tsp. salt
4 large eggs
1/2 cup buttermilk
1 tsp. vanilla extract

for the frosting
1/2 cup (1 stick) sweet butter, softened
2 cups confectioners' sugar, sifted
1 tsp. vanilla extract
2 tsp. pale dry sherry
4 tbsp. sweetened coconut

Preheat the oven to 350°F (175°C). Place 18 paper baking cups in muffin pans. Combine all the cupcake ingredients in a large bowl and beat with an electric mixer until smooth and pale, about 2 to 3 minutes. Spoon the batter into the cups. Bake for 20 minutes. Remove pans from the oven and cool for 5 minutes. Then remove the cupcakes and cool on a rack.

For the frosting, beat the butter, confectioners' sugar, vanilla, and sherry in a medium bowl until smooth and creamy. Spread on top of the cupcakes. Sprinkle a little coconut on top to resemble snowflakes.

Store unfrosted in an airtight container for up to 3 days, or freeze for up to 3 months.

Makes 1 1/2 dozen

independence day cupcakes

see variations page 171

With their red, white, and blue frosting, these cupcakes make for a festive Fourth of July!

for the cupcakes
1 cup (2 sticks) sweet butter, softened
1 cup granulated sugar
2 cups cake flour
2 tsp. baking powder
1 tsp. salt
4 large eggs
1/2 cup buttermilk
1 tsp. vanilla extract

for the frosting
1/2 cup (1 stick) sweet butter, softened
2 cups confectioners' sugar, sifted
1 tsp. vanilla extract
6 oz. ready-to-roll white fondant frosting
Red food coloring
Blue food coloring

Preheat the oven to 350°F (175°C). Place 18 paper baking cups in muffin pans. Combine all the cupcake ingredients in a large bowl and beat with an electric mixer until smooth and pale, about 2 to 3 minutes. Spoon the batter into the cups. Bake for 20 minutes. Remove pans from the oven and cool for 5 minutes. Then remove the cupcakes and cool on a rack.

To make the frosting, beat the butter and confectioners' sugar until soft. Add the vanilla and beat again. Spread onto the cooled cupcakes. Divide fondant into thirds. In one bowl, color one third with red coloring. In a second bowl, color another third blue. Roll white fondant to 1/8 in. (3 mm) thick. Cut out 18 circles using a 2 1/2-in. (6-cm) cookie cutter and lay on top of the frosted cupcakes. Roll out red and blue fondant to 1/8 in. (3 mm) thick. Cut out stars and thin stripes of the colors and lay them on white fondant, mimicking the look of the American flag. Store unfrosted in an airtight container for up to 3 days.

Makes 1 1/2 dozen

love-heart cupcakes

see variations page 172

These cupcakes make a delightful romantic gift for your true love on Valentine's Day — don't forget to attach a lover's message!

for the cupcakes
1 cup (2 sticks) sweet butter, softened
1 cup granulated sugar
2 cups cake flour
2 tsp. baking powder
1 tsp. salt
4 large eggs

1/2 cup buttermilk
1 tsp. vanilla extract

for the frosting
4 oz. ready-to-roll fondant frosting
Red food coloring
3 tbsp. raspberry jam
Silver candy balls

Preheat the oven to 350°F (175°C). Dust two cookie sheets with confectioners' sugar and put aside. Place 18 paper baking cups in muffin pans. Combine all the cupcake ingredients in a large bowl and beat with an electric mixer until smooth and pale, about 2 to 3 minutes. Spoon the batter into the cups. Bake for 20 minutes. Remove pans from the oven and cool for 5 minutes. Then remove cupcakes and cool on a rack.

To make the frosting, divide the fondant in half. In one bowl, color one half with red food coloring. Roll the white fondant frosting to 1/8 in. (3 mm) thick. Cut 18 circles using a 2 1/2-in. (6-cm) cookie cutter, and set them on one of the cookie sheets. Roll the red fondant frosting to 1/8 in. (3 mm) thick. Using a heart-shaped cutter, cut out 18 small hearts and set them on the other cookie sheet. Brush each cupcake with a little jam and lay a white circle on top. Place a heart on top of the circle. Decorate with silver balls around the edge. Store unfrosted in an airtight container for up to 3 days, or freeze for up to 3 months.

Makes 1 1/2 dozen

birthday cupcakes

see variations page 173

This is an easy and fun way to personalize birthday cupcakes!

for the cupcakes
1 cup (2 sticks) sweet butter, softened
1 cup granulated sugar
2 cups cake flour
2 tsp. baking powder
1 tsp. salt
4 large eggs
1/2 cup buttermilk
1 tsp. vanilla extract

for the frosting
1/2 cup (1 stick) sweet butter, softened
2 cups confectioners' sugar, sifted
1 tsp. vanilla extract
6 oz. ready-to-roll white fondant frosting
Red food coloring
Blue food coloring
Silver candy balls

Preheat the oven to 350°F (175°C). Place 18 paper baking cups in muffin pans. Combine all the cupcake ingredients in a large bowl and beat with an electric mixer until smooth and pale, about 2 to 3 minutes. Spoon the batter into the cups. Bake for 20 minutes. Remove pans from the oven and cool for 5 minutes. Then remove the cupcakes and cool on a rack.

For the frosting, beat the butter and confectioners' sugar in a medium bowl until soft and creamy. Add the vanilla and beat again. Spread onto the cooled cupcakes. Divide the fondant frosting into thirds. In a bowl, color one third with red food coloring. In a second bowl, color another third with blue food coloring. Roll the white fondant to 1/8 in. (3 mm) thick. Cut 18 circles using a 2 1/2-in. (6-cm) cookie cutter. Lay on top of the frosted cupcakes. Roll the red and blue fondant to 1/8 in. (3 mm) thick. Using mini alphabet cookie cutters, cut out initials and decorate the cupcakes. Garnish with silver balls.

Makes 1 1/2 dozen

easter egg nests

see base recipe page 149

silver egg nests
Prepare the basic cupcake recipe, substituting 54 silver candy-coated almonds for the candy eggs.

orange-flavored egg nests
Prepare the basic cupcake recipe, adding 1 teaspoon orange extract to the chocolate frosting.

chocolate chip egg nests
Prepare the basic cupcake recipe, folding 1/2 cup (3 1/2 oz.) semisweet chocolate chips into the batter.

easter egg baskets
Prepare the basic cupcake recipe. In place of chopped chocolate, use sweetened, flaked coconut colored with green food coloring. Bend a pipe cleaner and attach to each cupcake as a basket handle.

jelly bean baskets
Prepare the basic cupcake recipe. In place of chopped chocolate, use sweetened, flaked coconut colored with green food coloring. Subtitute jelly beans for mini chocolate eggs. Bend a pipe cleaner and attach to each cupcake as a basket handle.

variations

wedding cupcakes

see base recipe page 150

primrose wedding cupcakes
Prepare the basic cupcake recipe, substituting 18 frosted primroses for the roses.

chocolate wedding cupcakes
Prepare the basic cupcake recipe, folding 1/2 cup (3 1/2 oz.) semisweet chocolate chips into the creamed batter.

amaretto wedding cupcakes
Drizzle 3 tablespoons Amaretto over the cooled cupcakes before frosting them.

rose petal wedding cupcakes
Prepare the basic cupcake recipe, substituting 2 cups (1/4 oz.) fresh, fragrant rose petals for the frosted roses and almonds.

elegant wedding cupcakes
Prepare the basic cupcake recipe, substituting 2 cups (1/4 oz.) fresh, fragrant white rose petals for the frosted roses and almonds. Frost the cupcakes, sprinkle with crystal sanding sugar, then top with rose petals.

variations

passover cupcakes

see base recipe page 152

cranberry passover cupcakes
Prepare the basic cupcake recipe, substituting 1 3/4 cups (6 oz.) fresh cranberries for the blueberries.

orange & raisin passover cupcakes
Prepare the basic cupcake recipe, substituting 1/2 cup (3 1/2 oz.) raisins for the blueberries. Add 1 teaspoon orange extract to the egg mixture.

lemon & ginger passover cupcakes
Prepare the basic cupcake recipe, substituting 1 tablespoon lemon zest and 3 tablespoons chopped candied ginger for the blueberries.

cherry & almond passover cupcakes
Prepare the basic cupcake recipe, substituting almond extract for the cinnamon and 1/2 cup (3 1/2 oz.) dried cherries for the blueberries.

date & almond passover cupcakes
Prepare the basic cupcake recipe, substituting almond extract for the cinnamon and 1/2 cup (2 1/2 oz.) dried chopped dates for the blueberries.

irish barm brack cupcakes

see base recipe page 153

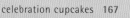

sugar-glazed barm brack cupcakes
Prepare the basic cupcake recipe. Prepare a glaze by mixing 2 tablespoons
boiling water with 1 tablespoon superfine sugar. Brush the glaze on the
cupcakes while they are still warm in the pan. Return the pan to the oven
for a few minutes to allow the glaze to set and turn a shiny brown.

whiskey-glazed barm brack cupcakes
Prepare the basic cupcake recipe. Prepare a glaze by mixing 2 tablespoons
warm Irish whiskey with 1 tablespoon superfine sugar. Brush the glaze on
the cupcakes while they are still warm in the pan. Return the pan to the
oven for a few minutes to allow the glaze to set and turn a shiny brown.

apricot barm brack cupcakes
Prepare the basic cupcake recipe, adding 1/2 cup (3 1/2 oz.) chopped
dried apricots to the dried fruit mixture. Increase quantity of black tea
to 1 1/4 cups (10 fl. oz.).

boston irish barm brack cupcakes
Prepare the basic cupcake recipe, adding 1/2 cup (3 1/2 oz.) semisweet
chocolate chips after creaming.

variations

king cupcakes

see base recipe page 154

raisin king cupcakes
Prepare the basic cupcake recipe, folding 1/2 cup (3 1/2 oz.) golden raisins into the creamed batter.

walnut king cupcakes
Prepare the basic cupcake recipe, folding 1/2 cup (3 1/2 oz.) chopped walnuts into the creamed batter.

white chocolate king cupcakes
Prepare the basic cupcake recipe, folding 1/2 cup (3 1/2 oz.) white chocolate chips into the creamed batter.

kwanza cupcakes
Prepare the basic cupcake recipe, substituting black and red sugars for yellow and purple.

baby shower cupcakes
Prepare the basic cupcake recipe. For the decoration, substitute pastel yellow, blue, green, and pink sugars in place of gold, green, and purple.

christmas tree cupcakes

see base recipe page 156

ginger & raisin christmas tree cupcakes
Prepare the basic cupcake recipe, adding 2 teaspoons ground ginger to
the cupcake ingredients, and folding 1/2 cup (3 1/2 oz.) raisins into the
creamed batter.

orange & lemon christmas tree cupcakes
Prepare the basic cupcake recipe, adding 1 tablespoon grated orange zest
and 1 tablespoon grated lemon zest to the creamed batter.

white chocolate christmas tree cupcakes
Prepare the basic cupcake recipe, folding 1/2 cup (3 1/2 oz.) white chocolate
chips into the creamed batter.

christmas ornament cupcakes
Prepare the basic cupcake recipe. Substitute cut-out circles, stars, and stripes
for Christmas trees and decorate the cupcakes.

easy christmas tree cupcakes
Prepare the basic recipe. For the decoration, substitute ready-made sugar
paste Christmas trees or tiny Christmas tree cookies for the colored fondant.

variations

snowflake cupcakes

see base recipe page 158

poppy seed snowflake cupcakes
Prepare the basic cupcake recipe, adding 2 tablespoons poppy seeds to the creamed batter.

mixed berry snowflake cupcakes
Prepare the basic cupcake recipe, folding 4 tablespoons dried mixed cranberries, cherries, and blueberries into the creamed batter.

hazelnut snowflake cupcakes
Prepare the basic cupcake recipe, folding 3 tablespoons roasted chopped hazelnuts into the creamed batter.

sparkly snowflake cupcakes
Prepare the basic cupcake recipe, sprinkling each cupcake with sparkly sanding sugar.

let-it-snow cupcakes
Prepare the basic cupcake recipe, sprinkling each cupcake with pearl sugar.

independence day cupcakes

see base recipe page 159

raisin independence day cupcakes
Prepare the basic cupcake recipe, folding 1/2 cup (3 1/2 oz.) raisins into the creamed batter.

white chocolate independence day cupcakes
Prepare the basic cupcake recipe, folding 1/2 cup (3 1/2 oz.) white chocolate chips into the creamed batter.

candied peel independence day cupcakes
Prepare the basic cupcake recipe, folding 2 tablespoons chopped candied peel into the creamed batter.

red, white & blueberry independence day cupcakes
Prepare the basic cupcake recipe. For the frosting, substitute prepared white frosting for the fondant. Decorate the cupcakes with 1 cup (4 1/2 oz.) sliced strawberries and 1 cup (4 1/2 oz.) whole blueberries.

sparkler cupcakes
Prepare the basic cupcake recipe. For the frosting, substitute prepared white frosting for the fondant. Decorate the cupcakes with sanding sugar and place a sparkler in the center of each.

variations

love-heart cupcakes

see base recipe page 161

white chocolate heart cupcakes
Prepare the basic cupcake recipe, folding 1/2 cup (3 1/2 oz.) white chocolate chips into the creamed batter.

macadamia nut heart cupcakes
Prepare the basic cupcake recipe, folding 1/2 cup (3 1/2 oz.) lightly toasted and chopped macadamia nuts into the creamed batter.

cherry heart cupcakes
Prepare the basic cupcake recipe, folding 4 tablespoons chopped candied cherries into the creamed batter.

raspberry heart cupcakes
Prepare the basic cupcake recipe, substituting prepared white frosting for fondant. Decorate with 2 cups (8 oz.) fresh raspberries.

be mine heart cupcakes
Prepare the basic cupcake recipe, substituting prepared white frosting for fondant. Decorate with 2 cups (10 oz.) valentine-themed heart candies.

variations

birthday cupcakes

see base recipe page 162

cherry & almond birthday cupcakes
Prepare the basic cupcake recipe, folding 2 tablespoons chopped candied cherries and 2 tablespoons chopped blanched almonds into the creamed batter.

orange birthday cupcakes
Prepare the basic cupcake recipe, adding 1 teaspoon orange extract to the creamed batter.

candied fruit birthday cupcakes
Prepare the basic cupcake recipe, folding 3 tablespoons chopped candied citrus fruits into the creamed batter.

happy birthday cupcakes
Prepare the basic cupcake recipe, substituting prepared white frosting for fondant. Decorate with colored sprinkles and place a small candle in the center of each cupcake.

cupcakes
for kids

Crisp rice cupcakes and mini peanut butter cupcakes

are a great way to get kids involved in the kitchen.

These cupcakes are so much fun to decorate, it can

be a party in itself!

s'more cupcakes

see variations page 195

Building s'more cupcakes is great fun for everyone. They require little fuss and effort, with a quick assembly and baking time.

24 graham crackers
7 oz. semisweet chocolate bars, broken into 12 squares
1/2 cup (3 1/2 oz.) chopped walnuts

3 tbsp. sweetened coconut
1 cup (2 oz.) mini marshmallows

Preheat the oven to 325°C (160°C). Place 12 paper baking cups in a muffin pan. Lay a graham cracker in the bottom of each cup. Add a piece of chocolate, followed by a sprinkle of walnuts and coconut. Lay another graham cracker on top.

Bake for 7 minutes, until the chocolate has melted. Remove pan from the oven. Push the graham cracker "lids" down so that they are secure.

Pop a couple of marshmallows on top of each cupcake. Return pan to the oven for 10 minutes, until the marshmallows melt and brown slightly.

Remove pan from the oven and cool for 5 minutes. Remove the cupcakes and cool on a rack.

Store in an airtight container for up to 24 hours.

Makes 1 dozen

toadstool cupcakes

see variations page 196

These funky toadstool cupcakes will brighten up any children's party. You can find white fondant frosting at cake decorating and baking supply stores.

for the cupcakes
1 cup (2 sticks) sweet butter, softened
1 cup granulated sugar
2 cups cake flour
2 tsp. baking powder
1 tsp. salt
4 large eggs
1/2 cup buttermilk
1 tsp. vanilla extract

for the frosting
3 cups confectioners' sugar, sifted
1 cup (2 sticks) sweet butter, softened
Pinch of salt
Red food coloring
2 oz. ready-to-roll white fondant frosting

Preheat the oven to 350°F (175°C). Place 18 paper baking cups in muffin pans. Combine all the cupcake ingredients in a large bowl and beat with an electric mixer until smooth and pale, about 2 to 3 minutes. Spoon the batter into the cups. Bake for 20 minutes. Remove pans from the oven and cool for 5 minutes. Then remove the cupcakes and cool on a rack.

To make the frosting, cream the confectioners' sugar, butter, and salt in a medium bowl with an electric mixer until smooth. Add a few drops of the food coloring, and mix until the frosting is a uniform bright red. Cut small circles out of the fondant icing. Spoon the red frosting onto the cupcakes and place the white fondant circles on top. Store unfrosted in an airtight container for up to 3 days, or freeze for up to 3 months.

Makes 1 1/2 dozen

ice cream cone cupcakes

see variations page 197

These cupcakes look like ice cream — but they won't melt!

for the cupcakes
1/2 cup (1 stick) sweet butter, softened
1/2 cup granulated sugar
1 cup cake flour
1 tsp. baking powder
1/2 tsp. salt
2 large eggs
1/4 cup buttermilk
1/2 tsp. vanilla extract
12 mini flat-bottomed wafer ice cream cones

for the frosting
1 1/2 cups confectioners' sugar, sifted
1/4 cup (1/2 stick) sweet butter, softened
Pinch of salt
1/4 cup heavy cream
1 tsp. vanilla extract
2 tbsp. colored sprinkles

Preheat the oven to 350°F (175°C). Line a 24-cup mini muffin pan with paper baking cups. Combine all the cupcake ingredients in a large bowl and beat with an electric mixer until smooth and pale, about 2 to 3 minutes. Spoon the batter into the cups. Bake for 20 minutes. Remove pan from the oven and cool for 5 minutes. Then remove the cupcakes and cool on a rack. Peel off the paper baking cups, and place the cupcakes inside the ice cream cones.

To make the frosting, beat the confectioners' sugar, butter, and salt using an electric mixer. Add the cream and vanilla, and beat until smooth. If loose, add more confectioners' sugar, until desired consistency is achieved. Pipe the mixture in a swirl on top of the cupcake. Shake some sprinkles on top.

Makes 2 dozen

think pink cupcakes

see variations page 198

Pink in name, pink in nature — these frosted cupcakes will brighten up any occasion!

for the cupcakes
1 cup (2 sticks) sweet butter, softened
1 cup granulated sugar
2 cups cake flour
2 tsp. baking powder
1 tsp. salt
4 large eggs
1/2 cup buttermilk
1 tsp. vanilla extract

for the frosting
3 cups confectioners' sugar, sifted
1 cup (2 sticks) sweet butter, softened
Pinch of salt
Pink food coloring
Silver candy balls

Preheat the oven to 350°F (175°C). Place 18 paper baking cups in muffin pans. Combine all the cupcake ingredients in a large bowl and beat with an electric mixer until smooth and pale, about 2 to 3 minutes.

Spoon the batter into the cups. Bake for 20 minutes. Remove pans from the oven and cool for 5 minutes. Then remove the cupcakes and cool on a rack.

To make the frosting, cream the confectioners' sugar, butter, and salt with an electric mixer until smooth. Add a few drops of food coloring, and mix well. Spread the frosting liberally onto the cooled cupcakes and sprinkle with silver balls.

Store unfrosted in an airtight container for up to 3 days, or freeze for up to 3 months.

Makes 1 1/2 dozen

cookies & cream cupcakes

see variations page 199

Mix crushed cookies into the batter to give a crispy crunch to these cupcakes.

for the cupcakes
1 cup (2 sticks) sweet butter, softened
1 cup granulated sugar
2 cups cake flour
2 tsp. baking powder
1 tsp. salt
4 large eggs
1/2 cup buttermilk

1 tsp. vanilla extract
10 crushed cream-filled chocolate cookies

for the frosting
3 cups confectioners' sugar, sifted
1 cup (2 sticks) sweet butter, softened
Pinch of salt
10 chopped cream-filled chocolate cookies

Preheat the oven to 350°F (175°C). Place 18 foil or paper baking cups in muffin pans. Combine all the cupcake ingredients, except the cookies, in a large bowl and beat with an electric mixer until smooth and pale, about 2 to 3 minutes. Stir in the cookies.

Spoon the batter into the cups. Bake for 20 minutes. Remove pans from the oven and cool for 5 minutes. Then remove the cupcakes and cool on a wire rack.

To make the frosting, beat the confectioners' sugar, butter, and salt using an electric mixer. Spread the frosting onto the cooled cupcakes and sprinkle the chopped cookies on top.

Store unfrosted in an airtight container for up to 3 days, or freeze for up to 3 months.

Makes 1 1/2 dozen

alphabet cupcakes

see variations page 200

Line these up to spell somebody's name at a birthday party! You can find ready-to-roll fondant at cake decorator's or cake supply shops. Or use gum candy alphabet letters.

for the cupcakes
1 cup (2 sticks) sweet butter, softened
1 cup granulated sugar
2 cups cake flour
2 tsp. baking powder
1 tsp. salt
4 large eggs
1/2 cup buttermilk
1 tsp. vanilla extract

for the frosting
12 oz. ready-to-roll white fondant frosting
3 tbsp. raspberry jam
Food coloring
Colored sprinkles

Preheat the oven to 350°F (175°C). Place 18 paper baking cups in muffin pans. Combine all the cupcake ingredients in a large bowl and beat with an electric mixer until smooth and pale, about 2 to 3 minutes. Spoon the batter into the cups. Bake for 20 minutes. Remove pans from the oven and cool for 5 minutes. Then remove the cupcakes and cool on a rack.

For the frosting, divide the fondant into 4 portions. In one bowl, color the fondant black; in a second bowl, color the fondant red; in a third bowl, color the fondant green. Roll out the white fondant and cut 18 circles using a 2-in. (5-cm) cookie cutter. Brush the cupcakes with a little of the jam. Press the circles onto the cupcakes. Roll out the remaining colored fondant. Using mini alphabet cutters, cut letter shapes from the colored fondant frosting and place them on top of the white circles. Sprinkle the edges with colored sprinkles.

Makes 1 1/2 dozen

pineapple cupcakes

see variations page 201

These cupcakes melt in the mouth and are the perfect teatime treat.

for the cupcakes
1 cup (2 sticks) sweet butter, softened
1 cup granulated sugar
2 cups cake flour
1 tsp. baking powder
4 eggs
1 tsp. vanilla extract
1 cup drained crushed pineapple

for the frosting
1 cup cream cheese, softened
1 1/2 cups confectioners' sugar, sifted
1 tbsp. lemon juice
1 tsp. vanilla extract
1/2 cup (3 1/2 oz.) chopped walnuts

Preheat the oven to 350°F (175°C). Place 18 paper baking cups in muffin pans. Combine all the cupcake ingredients, except the pineapple, in a large bowl and beat with an electric mixer for about 2 to 3 minutes. Stir in the pineapple. Spoon the batter into the cups. Bake for 20 minutes. Remove pans from the oven and cool for 5 minutes. Then remove the cupcakes and cool on a rack. To make the frosting, slowly beat the cream cheese and confectioners' sugar in a large bowl with an electric mixer until creamy and soft. Add the lemon juice and vanilla, and beat briskly until well combined. Spread the frosting onto the cooled cupcakes and garnish with the chopped walnuts.

Store unfrosted in an airtight container for 2 to 3 days, or freeze for up to 3 months.

Makes 1 1/2 dozen

mini peanut butter cupcakes

see variations page 202

Simple and no fuss. You can make these cupcakes in large batches, which makes them ideal for kids' parties and picnics.

2 1/2 cups milk chocolate chips
2 tbsp. sweet butter
3 tbsp. heavy cream
1 cup smooth peanut butter

Place 12 mini foil baking cups in a muffin pan.

Place the chocolate, butter, and cream in a double boiler or in a medium bowl over a pan of simmering water, and stir until smooth. Remove from the heat and set aside.

With damp hands, shape the peanut butter into 12 small flat circles. Push the peanut butter into the bottom of the cups.

Pour the melted chocolate over the peanut butter, and refrigerate for at least 2 hours.

Store in an airtight container for up to 3 days.

Makes 1 dozen

crisp rice cupcakes

see variations page 203

I'm not too sure how many will reach the table, but these simple no-bake cupcakes are great fun for the budding young chef to try.

1 cup (7 oz.) semisweet chocolate chips
1/4 cup (1/2 stick) sweet butter, softened
5 tbsp. corn syrup
3 cups (3 1/2 oz.) crisp rice cereal

Place 12 foil or paper baking cups on a tray.

Place the chocolate and butter in a double boiler or in a medium bowl over a pan of simmering water, and stir until melted.

Remove pan from the heat and stir in the corn syrup and cereal. Drop spoonfuls of the mixture into the cups.

Refrigerate for 1 hour before serving.

Store in an airtight container for up to 5 days.

Makes 1 dozen

eggy cupcakes

see variations page 204

Don't worry — you won't have to crack whole eggs to get this lovely sunny-side-up look.
Serve these cupcakes for breakfast with a glass of freshly squeezed juice.

for the cupcakes
1 cup (2 sticks) sweet butter, softened
1 cup granulated sugar
2 cups cake flour
2 tsp. baking powder
1 tsp. salt
4 large eggs
1/2 cup buttermilk
1 tsp. vanilla extract

for the frosting
3 cups confectioners' sugar, sifted
1 cup (2 sticks) sweet butter, softened
Pinch of salt
18 drained canned peach halves

Preheat the oven to 350°F (175°C). Place 18 paper baking cups in muffin pans. Combine all
the cupcake ingredients in a large bowl and beat with an electric mixer until smooth and
pale, about 2 to 3 minutes. Spoon the batter into the cups. Bake for 20 minutes. Remove
pans from the oven and cool for 5 minutes. Then remove the cupcakes and cool on a rack.

To make the frosting, put the confectioners' sugar, butter, and salt in a large bowl and beat
with an electric mixer until smooth. Liberally spread the frosting onto the cooled cupcakes
and garnish each cupcake with a peach half.

Store unfrosted in an airtight container for up to 3 days, or freeze for up to 3 months.

Makes 1 1/2 dozen

chocolate berry cupcakes

see variations page 205

My good friend Beverley Glock gave me this recipe. She runs a company called "Splat," which organizes children's parties where both children and adults can bake.

for the cupcakes
1/2 cup fresh or thawed frozen blackberries
3 tbsp. water
1 cup granulated sugar
1 cup cake flour
1 tsp. baking powder
1/2 tsp. salt
1/2 cup soft margarine

2 large eggs
1 tbsp. Dutch-process cocoa powder

for the ganache
3/4 cup (5 oz.) broken bittersweet chocolate
3/4 cup heavy cream
12 blackberries

Preheat the oven to 350°F (175°C). Line a 12-cup mini muffin pan with paper baking cups. Combine the blackberries, water, and 1/2 cup sugar in a small saucepan over low heat. Simmer for about 5 minutes, until the fruit starts to release its juices. Set aside to cool. Combine the rest of the ingredients in a medium bowl and beat with an electric mixer until pale and creamy, about 2 to 3 minutes. Spoon the batter into the cups. Spoon a little of the fruit on top and divide evenly among cupcakes. Bake for 20 minutes. Remove the pan and cool for 5 minutes. Then remove the cupcakes and cool on a rack. Store in an airtight container for up to 2 days, or freeze for up to 3 months.

To make the ganache before serving, melt the chocolate and cream in a double boiler over low heat, until glossy and smooth. Dollop a spoonful of ganache onto each cooled cupcake and top with a blackberry. Refrigerate until set, then serve.

Makes 1 dozen small cupcakes

pop rocks cupcakes

see variations page 206

Try these for a kids' party and watch their faces as the candy explodes in their mouths!

for the cupcakes
1 cup (2 sticks) sweet butter, softened
1 cup granulated sugar
2 cups cake flour
2 tsp. baking powder
1 tsp. salt
4 large eggs
1/2 cup buttermilk
1 tsp. vanilla extract

for the frosting
1/2 cup (1 stick) sweet butter, softened
2 cups confectioners' sugar, sifted
1 tsp. vanilla extract
2 packages fruit-flavored Pop Rocks

Preheat the oven to 350°F (175°C). Place 18 paper baking cups in muffin pans. Combine all cupcake ingredients in a large bowl and beat with an electric mixer until smooth and pale, about 2 to 3 minutes. Spoon the batter into the cups. Bake for 20 minutes.

Remove pans from the oven and cool for 5 minutes. Then remove the cupcakes and cool on a rack.

To make the frosting, cream the butter, confectioners' sugar, and vanilla in a medium bowl until smooth. Smear onto the cupcakes and sprinkle with Pop Rocks candy.

Store unfrosted in an airtight container for up to 2 days, or freeze for up to 3 months.

Makes 1 1/2 dozen

jelly donut cupcakes

see variations page 207

These cupcakes aren't donuts, but I'm sure you'll see the likeness when you bite into one.

for the cupcakes
1 cup (2 sticks) sweet butter, softened
1 cup granulated sugar
2 cups cake flour
1 tsp. baking powder
4 eggs
1 tsp. vanilla extract
1/2 cup raspberry jelly or jam

for the frosting
1 cup cream cheese, softened
1 1/2 cups confectioners' sugar, sifted
1 tbsp. lemon juice
1 tsp. vanilla extract

Preheat the oven to 350°F (175°C). Place 18 paper baking cups in muffin pans. Combine all the cupcake ingredients, except the jelly, in a large bowl and beat with an electric mixer, about 2 to 3 minutes. Spoon the batter into the cups. Bake for 20 minutes. Remove pans from the oven and cool for 5 minutes. Then remove the cupcakes and cool on a rack.

Slice the top off each cupcake, hollow out a small hole with a teaspoon, and fill with the jelly. Replace the top. To make the frosting, slowly beat the cream cheese and confectioners' sugar in a large bowl with an electric mixer until creamy and soft. Add the lemon juice and vanilla, and beat briskly until well combined. Spread the frosting onto the cupcakes.

Store unfrosted in an airtight container for up to 2 days, or freeze for up to 3 months.

Makes 1 1/2 dozen

s'more cupcakes

see base recipe page 175

pecan s'more cupcakes
Prepare the basic cupcake recipe, substituting 1/2 cup (3 1/2 oz.) roughly chopped pecans for the walnuts.

white chocolate s'more cupcakes
Prepare the basic cupcake recipe, substituting 1/4 cup (2 oz.) white chocolate chips for half the semisweet chocolate.

chocolate & raspberry s'more cupcakes
Prepare the basic cupcake recipe. Add 1/2 cup (2 oz.) lightly crushed raspberries along with the coconut and walnuts.

banana s'more cupcakes
Prepare the basic cupcake recipe, substituting 1 fresh sliced banana for the walnuts.

strawberry s'more cupcakes
Prepare the basic cupcake recipe, substituting 1 cup (4 oz.) fresh sliced strawberries for the walnuts.

toadstool cupcakes

see base recipe page 177

koala bear cupcakes

Prepare the basic cupcake recipe. Omit the rolled fondant. Color the frosting
with brown food coloring instead of red. Make a koala face on each cupcake:
A chocolate-covered Brazil nut for the nose, 2 walnut halves for ears, and
2 candy eyes.

sneaky snake cupcakes

Prepare the basic cupcake recipe. For the frosting, substitute 2 oz. green
ready-rolled fondant frosting for the white fondant. Brush each cupcake
with a little fruit jelly. Roll the green fondant thinly and, using a cookie
cutter, cut 18 circles 2-1/2 in. (6-cm) across and place one on each cupcake.
For the trees, cut 6 chocolate sticks into 3 sections 2-in. (5-cm) in length,
and stand upright on the fondant frosting. Roll 2 oz. red fondant frosting
into 18 sausages 6-in. (15-cm) in length. Curl the fondant around the
chocolate "trees" and decorate with candy-eyes.

bling cupcakes

Prepare the basic cupcake recipe. Omit the rolled fondant. Decorate the red
frosting on the cupcakes with silver and gold candy balls.

ice cream cone cupcakes

see base recipe page 178

chocolate-frosted cone cupcakes
Prepare the basic cupcake recipe. To the frosting, add 1/2 cup (3 1/2 oz.) chocolate chips along with the cream and vanilla.

choc & mint-frosted cone cupcakes
Prepare the basic cupcake recipe. To the frosting, add 1/2 cup (3 1/2 oz.) mint chocolate chips along with the cream. Substitute 1 teaspoon mint extract for the vanilla.

honey & cream-frosted cone cupcakes
Prepare the basic cupcake recipe. To the frosting, add 1/3 (4 oz.) cup honey after creaming the confectioners' sugar and butter.

strawberry ice cream cone cupcakes
Prepare the basic cupcake recipe. For the frosting, substitute 1/2 cup (2 oz.) mashed fresh strawberries for the cream. Decorate with a strawberry on top of each cone.

caramel apple ice cream cone cupcakes
Prepare the basic cupcake recipe. For the frosting, substitute 1/2 cup (4 fl. oz.) apple juice for the cream. Drizzle each cone with prepared caramel ice cream sauce.

variations

think pink cupcakes

see base recipe page 181

azure cupcakes
Prepare the basic cupcake recipe. For the frosting, substitute blue food coloring for pink, and top with blue azure sugar crystals.

lavender sugar cupcakes
Prepare the basic cupcake recipe. For the frosting, substitute blue food coloring for pink. Make lavender sugar by combining 3 tablespoons lavender flowers and 3/4 cup (5 oz.) superfine sugar in a food processor for about 2 minutes. Put the sugar in a cool dry place, and let the flavors mingle for about 2 hours. Sprinkle on top of the frosting.

rose sugar cupcakes
Prepare the basic cupcake recipe. Make rose-petal sugar by combining 3 tablespoons red rose petals and 3/4 cup (5 oz.) superfine sugar in a food processor for about 2 minutes. Put the sugar in a cool dry place, and let the flavors mingle for about 2 hours. Sprinkle on top of the frosting.

pink lemonade cupcakes
Prepare the basic cupcake recipe. For the frosting, add 1 tablespoon sugar-free pink lemonade drink mix.

cookies & cream cupcakes

see base recipe page 182

minted cookies & cream cupcakes
Prepare the basic cupcake recipe, using cream-filled mint chocolate cookies in both the cupcakes and the frosting.

graham crackers & cream cupcakes
Prepare the basic cupcake recipe, substituting 1/2 cup (3 1/2 oz.) crushed graham crackers for 10 cookies in the cupcakes, and another 1/2 cup (3 1/2 oz.) crushed graham crackers for the cookies in the frosting.

chocolate, nougat & cream cupcakes
Prepare the basic cupcake recipe, substituting 1/2 cup (3 1/2 oz.) chopped Baby Ruth bars for 10 cookies in the cupcakes, and another 1/2 cup (3 1/2 oz.) chopped Baby Ruth bars for the cookies in the frosting.

peanut butter cookies & cream cupcakes
Prepare the basic cupcake recipe, using peanut butter cookies in both the cupcakes and the frosting. Substitute 1/2 cup (3 oz.) creamy peanut butter for 1 stick butter in the frosting.

variations

alphabet cupcakes

see base recipe page 184

white chocolate alphabet cupcakes
Prepare the basic cupcake recipe, adding 1/2 cup (3 1/2 oz.) white chocolate chips to the creamed batter.

raisin alphabet cupcakes
Prepare the basic cupcake recipe, adding 1/2 cup (3 1/2 oz.) raisins to the creamed batter.

number cupcakes
Prepare the basic cupcake recipe. Use mini number cookie cutters instead of alphabet cutters.

easy alphabet cupcakes
Prepare the basic cupcake recipe. For the frosting, substitute prepared white frosting. Decorate with 10 oz. bag Gummi candy alphabet letters.

big number cupcakes
Prepare the basic cupcake recipe. For the frosting, substitute prepared white frosting. On wax or parchment paper, trace a circle the circumference of the cupcake top. Trace and cut out a number in the center of the paper. Place the stencil on top of the frosted cupcake and sprinkle colored sugar to create the number.

pineapple cupcakes

see base recipe page 185

kicked-up chile pineapple cupcakes
Prepare the basic cupcake recipe. Add 1 teaspoon seeded and finely chopped chile pepper to the creamed batter.

orange & pineapple cupcakes
Prepare the basic cupcake recipe. Add 2 tablespoons orange zest to the creamed batter.

coconut & pineapple cupcakes
Prepare the basic cupcake recipe. Add 1/2 cup (2 1/2 oz.) sweetened shredded coconut to the mixture after it has been creamed.

pineapple & marshmallow cupcakes
Prepare the basic cupcake recipe. Add 1/2 cup (1 oz.) colored miniature marshmallows to the mixture after it has been creamed.

pineapple & chocolate chip cupcakes
Prepare the basic cupcake recipe. Add 1/2 cup (3 oz.) chocolate chips to the mixture after it has been creamed.

mini peanut butter cupcakes

see base recipe page 186

mini marshmallow & peanut butter cupcakes
Prepare the basic cupcake recipe. Add 1 cup (2 oz.) chopped large
marshmallows to the melted chocolate mixture.

mini coconut & peanut butter cupcakes
Prepare the basic cupcake recipe. Add 3 tablespoons sweetened coconut to
the melted chocolate.

mini jam & peanut butter cupcakes
Prepare the basic cupcake recipe. Place a teaspoon of your favorite fruit jam
into the bottom of the baking cups and top with the peanut butter and then
the chocolate.

layered marshmallow & peanut butter cupcakes
Prepare the basic cupcake recipe. Place 2 miniature marshmallows into
the bottom of the baking cups and top with the peanut butter and then
the chocolate.

crisp rice cupcakes

see base recipe page 189

marshmallow & crisp rice cupcakes
Prepare the basic cupcake recipe. Stir in 1/2 cup (1 oz.) mini marshmallows along with the cereal.

raisins & crisp rice cupcakes
Prepare the basic cupcake recipe. Stir in 1/2 cup (3 1/2 oz.) raisins along with the cereal.

cherry & crisp rice cupcakes
Prepare the basic cupcake recipe. Stir in 1/2 cup (3 1/2 oz.) chopped red candied cherries along with the cereal.

bird's nest cupcakes
Prepare the basic cupcake recipe. Drop spoonfuls of the mixture into the cups, then make a nest shape with the spoon. Fill each nest with tiny colored sugar balls.

variations

eggy cupcakes

see base recipe page 190

kiwi cupcakes
Prepare the basic cupcake recipe, substituting 18 thin slices kiwi fruit for the peach halves.

nectarine cupcakes
Prepare the basic cupcake recipe, substituting 18 nectarine halves for the peach halves.

custard (runny egg) cupcakes
Prepare the basic cupcake recipe. Slice a thin circle off the top of each cooled cupcake. Using a teaspoon, make a small hole about 1 in. (2 1/2 cm) deep. Pipe 1 teaspoon prepared custard into the hole. Replace the "lid," frost and add the peach half.

hit-the-target cupcakes
Prepare the basic cupcake recipe. On wax or parchment paper, trace a circle the circumference of the cupcake top. Trace and cut out a circle in the center of the paper. Place the stencil on top of the frosted cupcake and sprinkle colored sugar to create the bull's-eye.

variations

chocolate berry cupcakes

see base recipe page 192

chocolate raspberry cupcakes
Prepare the basic cupcake recipe, substituting 1/2 cup (2 1/2 oz.) fresh raspberries for the blackberries.

chocolate blueberry cupcakes
Prepare the basic cupcake recipe, substituting 1/2 cup (2 oz.) fresh blueberries for the blackberries.

chocolate cherry cupcakes
Prepare the basic cupcake recipe, substituting 1/2 cup (2 oz.) fresh cherries for the blackberries.

chocolate strawberry cupcakes
Prepare the basic cupcake recipe, substituting strawberries for the blackberries.

variations

pop rocks cupcakes

see base recipe page 193

ginger pop rocks cupcakes
Prepare the basic cupcake recipe, adding 1 teaspoon ground ginger and
3 tablespoons candied ginger to the creamed cupcake batter.

cherry pop rocks cupcakes
Prepare the basic cupcake recipe, adding 1/2 cup (3 1/2 oz.) chopped candied
cherries to the creamed cupcake batter.

pineapple pop rocks cupcakes
Prepare the basic cupcake recipe, adding 1/2 cup (3 1/2 oz.) chopped dried
pineapple to the creamed cupcake batter.

strawberry surprise pop rocks cupcakes
Prepare the basic cupcake recipe, dropping 1 teaspoon of strawberry jam
in the center of each cupcake before baking. Use strawberry Pop Rocks on
the frosting.

variations

jelly donut cupcakes

see base recipe page 194

boston cream donut cupcakes
Prepare the basic cupcake recipe. Substitute 1/2 cup (4 fl. oz.) vanilla custard or pie filling for the raspberry jelly.

chocolate custard donut cupcakes
Prepare the basic cupcake recipe. Substitute 1/2 cup (4 fl. oz.) chocolate custard or pie filling for the raspberry jelly.

marmalade donut cupcakes
Prepare the basic cupcake recipe. Substitute 1/2 cup (5 oz.) orange marmalade for the raspberry jelly.

peanut butter & jelly donut cupcakes
Prepare the basic cupcake recipe. For the frosting, substitute creamy peanut butter for the cream cheese.

cupcakes for alternative diets

Wholesome, moist, and sweet banana and honey cupcakes, dairy-free berry cupcakes, gluten-free pecan cupcakes, and chocolate vegan cupcakes — anyone with special dietary requirements will be well catered for with the selection of recipes in this chapter.

mini couscous cupcakes

see variations page 234

Couscous, the world's smallest pasta, is a staple throughout northern Africa. It gives these cupcakes a light and elegant texture.

1/2 cup couscous
1/2 cup boiling water
2 cups all-purpose flour
2 tbsp. granulated sugar
1 tbsp. baking powder
Pinch of salt
1 tsp. toasted cumin seeds

1 tsp. ground coriander
1 large egg
4 tbsp. olive oil
1 tbsp. lemon zest
2 tbsp. chopped flat-leaf parsley

Preheat the oven to 350°F (175°C). Place 24 mini paper cups in a muffin pan. Put the couscous in a medium bowl and pour the boiling water over it. Cover and leave for 5 minutes, so the grains absorb the liquid. Fluff the grains apart with a fork.

Mix the dry ingredients in a bowl with a spoon. Beat the egg and oil in a large bowl with an electric mixer until combined. Add the couscous and the dry ingredients and mix until nearly combined. Fold in the lemon zest and parsley. Spoon the mixture into the cups. Bake for 20 minutes. Remove pan from the oven and cool for 5 minutes. Then remove the cupcakes and cool on a rack.

Store in an airtight container for up to 3 days, or freeze for up to 3 months.

Makes 2 dozen mini cupcakes

basil pesto cupcakes

see variations page 235

These unusually savory cupcakes make an ideal wholesome treat.

for the cupcakes
3/4 cup yellow cornmeal
1 cup all-purpose flour
2 tsp. baking powder
3 tbsp. sugar
Pinch of salt
2 large eggs

1 cup whole milk
4 tbsp. (1/2 stick) sweet butter, melted

for the frosting
1/2 cup basil pesto
1 1/2 cups cream cheese, softened
12 cherry tomatoes

Preheat the oven to 350°F (175°C). Place 12 paper baking cups into a muffin pan. In a medium bowl, stir the dry ingredients. Beat the eggs, milk, and butter in a large bowl with an electric mixer until combined. Add the flour mixture to the egg mixture, and stir until just combined. Spoon the batter into the cups. Bake for 20 minutes. Remove pan and cool for 5 minutes. Then remove the cupcakes and cool on a rack.

For the frosting, beat the pesto and cream cheese with an electric mixer until smooth and creamy. Smear the frosting onto the cooled cupcakes and top with the cherry tomatoes.

Store unfrosted in an airtight container for up to 3 days, or freeze for up to 3 months.

Makes 1 dozen

pb & banana cupcakes

see variations page 236

This familiar combination makes a truly delicious cupcake.

for the cupcake
1 cup (2 sticks) sweet butter, softened
1 cup granulated sugar
2 cups cake flour
2 tsp. baking powder
1 tsp. salt
4 large eggs
1/2 cup buttermilk
3 tbsp. ground almonds
1 tsp. vanilla extract

2 tsp. cinnamon
4 tbsp. peanut butter chips
1 cup (about 2) mashed bananas

for the frosting
1 cup cream cheese, softened
1 1/2 cups confectioners' sugar, sifted
1 tbsp. lemon juice
1 tsp. vanilla extract
1/2 cup mashed banana

Preheat the oven to 350°F (175°C). Place 24 paper baking cups in muffin pans. Combine the butter, sugar, flour, baking powder, salt, eggs, buttermilk, almonds, vanilla, and cinnamon in a large bowl and beat with an electric mixer until smooth and pale, about 2 to 3 minutes. Stir in the peanut butter chips and mashed banana. Spoon the batter into the paper cups. Bake for 20 minutes. Remove pan and cool for 5 minutes. Then remove the cupcakes and cool on a rack. To make the frosting, beat the cream cheese and confectioners' sugar in a medium bowl with an electric mixer until soft and light. Add the lemon juice, vanilla, and mashed bananas. Beat until well combined. Spoon the frosting over the cupcakes.

Store unfrosted in an airtight container for up to 2 days or freeze for up to 3 months.

Makes 2 dozen

ricotta cheesecake cupcakes

see variations page 237

Ricotta cheese is lower in fat than cream cheese and it has a great texture.

1 cup graham cracker crumbs
3 tbsp. margarine, melted
2 tbsp. honey
4 cups part-skim ricotta cheese
4 large eggs

1 1/2 cups confectioners' sugar, sifted
1 tsp. orange extract
1/2 cup (3 1/2 oz.) walnut halves

Preheat the oven to 325°F (160°C). Place 12 baking cups in a muffin pan.

In a food processor, combine the cracker crumbs, margarine, and honey. Spoon 1 tablespoon of the mixture into each cup, pressing firmly into the bottom. Chill until set.

In a large bowl, beat the ricotta with an electric mixer until soft. Then beat in the eggs, confectioners' sugar, and orange extract. Spoon the mixture into the cups. Place a walnut on top of each cupcake.

Bake for 25 minutes. Remove pan from the oven and cool for 5 minutes. Then remove the cupcakes and cool on a rack. Chill until ready to serve.

Store covered in the refrigerator for up to 2 days.

Makes 1 dozen

low-fat vanilla cupcakes

see variations page 238

After you have used the seeds from the vanilla bean, put the pod into an airtight jar and pour granulated sugar on top. In a few weeks you will have vanilla sugar!

for the cupcakes
3 large egg yolks
1 cup granulated sugar
1 vanilla bean, pod removed
1/4 cup cold water
1 cup cake flour
1 tsp. baking powder
Pinch of salt

5 large egg whites
1/8 tsp. cream of tartar

for the glaze
1 1/2 cups confectioners' sugar
1 tsp. vanilla extract
2 tbsp. lemon juice
1 tbsp. poppy seeds

Preheat the oven to 350°F (175°C). Place 12 paper baking cups in a muffin pan. In a large bowl, beat the egg yolks and half the sugar until pale and creamy. Then add the vanilla seeds. Add the water, flour, baking powder and salt to the egg mixture and beat with an electric mixer until just combined. In a medium bowl, combine the egg whites and cream of tartar. Beat with an electric mixer until soft peaks form. Add the remaining sugar, one-third at a time, beating well after each addition. Using a metal spoon, gently fold the egg whites into the batter. Spoon the mixture into the cups. Bake for 20 minutes. Remove and cool slightly. To make the glaze, sift the confectioners' sugar in a bowl. Add the vanilla extract, lemon juice, and poppy seeds and beat until creamy and slightly runny. Drizzle the glaze over warm cupcakes.

Store in an airtight container for up to 2 days, or freeze for up to 3 months.

Makes 1 dozen

flour-lite chocolate cupcakes

see variations page 239

This recipe has only a small amount of flour to give the cupcakes a light, fluffy texture.

1/2 cup Dutch-process cocoa powder
3/4 cup packed light brown sugar
3 tbsp. all-purpose flour
Pinch of salt
1 tsp. vanilla extract
1 tsp. orange extract
3/4 cup fat-free milk

1 cup chopped bittersweet chocolate
1 large egg, lightly beaten
3 large egg whites
1/4 tsp. cream of tartar
1/3 cup granulated sugar
Cocoa powder, for dusting
Confectioners' sugar, for dusting

In a heavy saucepan, combine the cocoa, sugar, flour, salt, vanilla, orange extract, and milk over a gentle heat. Stir until the sugar dissolves, being careful not to burn the mixture. Remove from the heat, and gradually stir in the chocolate until it melts. Whisk in the egg. Transfer to a large bowl to cool, and set aside. Preheat the oven to 350°F (175°C). Place 12 paper baking cups in a muffin pan. In a medium bowl, combine the egg whites and cream of tartar. Beat with an electric mixer until soft peaks form. Gradually add the sugar, one-third at a time, beating for 1 minute after each addition. Using a metal spoon, fold the egg whites into the chocolate, making sure not to overmix. Spoon the mixture into the cups. Bake for 20 minutes.

Remove the pan from the oven and cool for 5 minutes. Then remove the cupcakes, dust with cocoa powder and confectioners' sugar, and serve immediately.

Makes 1 dozen

quick applesauce cupcakes

see variations page 240

Simple to make and low in fat, this recipe is based on the classic streusel cake.

for the cupcakes
1/2 cup (1 stick) margarine, softened
3/4 cup packed light brown sugar
1 large egg, lightly beaten
3/4 cup unsweetened applesauce
2 cups cake flour
1 tsp. baking powder
1 tsp. ground ginger
1/4 tsp. ground cloves

for the topping
2 tbsp. margarine, softened
1/4 cup confectioners' sugar, sifted
3 tbsp. chopped walnuts
2 tbsp. rolled oats
2 tbsp. all-purpose flour
1/2 tsp. cinnamon

Preheat the oven to 350°F (175°C). Place 12 paper baking cups in a muffin pan. In a medium bowl, beat the margarine and sugar with an electric mixer until pale and creamy. Slowly add the egg and then the applesauce, beating well after each addition. Add the flour, baking powder, and spices, mixing until just combined. To make the topping, combine all the ingredients in a small bowl. Mix with a fork until the topping resembles coarse breadcrumbs. Set aside. Spoon the batter into the cups. Sprinkle some topping on each cupcake and bake for 20 to 25 minutes. Remove pan from the oven and cool for 5 minutes. Then remove the cupcakes and cool on a rack.

Store in an airtight container for up to 3 days, or freeze for up to 3 months.

Makes 1 dozen

glazed blueberry-lime cupcakes

see variations page 241

Low in fat with super-food blueberries — you may feel virtuous when you bake these!

for the cupcakes
1/2 cup (1 stick) margarine, softened
1 cup granulated sugar
2 large eggs, lightly beaten
1 tsp. vanilla extract
1/2 cup fat-free milk
2 cups cake flour
1 tsp. baking powder
1/2 tsp. salt

1 cup fresh blueberries
1 tbsp. grated lime zest

for the glaze
1/2 cup granulated sugar
2 tbsp. grated lime zest
3 tbsp. lime juice
2 tbsp. boiling water

Preheat the oven to 350°F (175°C). Place 18 paper baking cups in muffin pans. Combine the margarine and sugar with an electric mixer until soft and creamy. Add the eggs slowly and mix well. Beat in the vanilla and milk. Sift the flour, baking powder, and salt, and stir into the batter until just combined. Fold in the blueberries and lime zest. Spoon the mixture into the cups. Bake for 20 minutes. Remove pans from the oven and cool for 5 minutes. Then remove the cupcakes and cool on a rack. To make the glaze, mix the sugar, lime zest, lime juice, and boiling water in a small saucepan. Bring to a gentle simmer over a medium heat, stirring to dissolve the sugar. Simmer uncovered for 5 minutes. Remove from the heat, cool slightly, and spoon over the cool cupcakes.

Store in an airtight container for up to 3 days, or unglazed in the freezer for up to 3 months.

Makes 1 1/2 dozen

banana & honey cupcakes

see variations page 242

Bananas lend themselves to natural sweeteners like maple syrup and honey. Add walnuts to offset the sweetness and to give the cupcakes a little crunch.

1 3/4 cups (about 4) mashed bananas
3/4 cup packed light brown sugar
1/4 cup honey
4 tbsp. margarine, melted

2 cups cake flour
1 tsp. baking powder
1/2 tsp. salt
3/4 cup (5 oz.) roughly chopped walnuts

Preheat the oven to 350°F (175°C). Place 18 paper baking cups in muffin pans.

In a large bowl, combine the bananas, sugar, honey, and margarine. Beat with an electric mixer until well blended. Slowly add the flour, baking powder, and salt, and mix well. Fold in the chopped walnuts.

Spoon the batter into the cups. Bake for 20 minutes. Remove pans from the oven and cool for 5 minutes. Remove the cupcakes and cool on a rack. Place each in a foil cup to display.

Store in an airtight container for up to 2 days, or freeze for up to 3 months.

Makes 1 1/2 dozen

marbled mini bundt cakes

see variations page 243

Bake these cakes in little bundt pans for a really extravagant-looking cupcake. You can also use ordinary muffin pans.

1/2 cup (1 stick) margarine, softened
1 cup granulated sugar
2 large eggs, lightly beaten
1 tsp. vanilla extract
2 cups all-purpose flour
1 tbsp. baking powder

3/4 cup fat-free milk
2 tbsp. Dutch-process cocoa powder
1/2 cup (3 1/2 oz.) finely chopped semisweet
   chocolate
Cocoa powder for dusting

Preheat the oven to 350°F (175°C). Grease 6 mini bundt pans or a large 6-cup muffin pan. In a large bowl, beat the margarine and sugar with an electric mixer until thick and pale. Slowly add the eggs and vanilla, beating well. Mix the flour and baking powder in a medium bowl. Add to the margarine mixture in thirds, alternating with the milk.

Divide the batter into two bowls. Fold the cocoa powder and chocolate into one of the bowls. Spoon a little plain batter into the bottom of each bundt pan, then spoon some chocolate batter on top. Continue until each pan is three-quarters full and there are 4 layers. Swirl the mixture in each cup using the point of a knife. Bake for 35 minutes. Remove pans from the oven and cool for 10 minutes. Then remove the bundt cakes and cool on a rack. Serve dusted with cocoa powder.

Store in an airtight container for up to 2 days.

Makes 1/2 dozen

low-fat carrot & nut cupcakes

see variations page 244

The low-fat version of the classic American cake. If you can't get fat-free cream cheese for the frosting, use fat-free plain yogurt.

for the cupcakes
2 cups cake flour
1 tsp. baking powder
1/2 tsp. salt
1/2 tsp. nutmeg
1 tsp. ground ginger
3/4 cup packed brown sugar
1/2 cup shredded carrots
1/2 cup roughly chopped walnuts
3/4 cup (1 or 2) mashed bananas

2 lightly beaten eggs
2/3 cup vegetable oil

for the frosting
1 cup fat-free cream cheese, softened
1 cup confectioners' sugar, sifted
1 tsp. vanilla extract
4 tbsp. chopped walnuts
12 walnut halves

Preheat the oven to 350°F (175°C). Place 12 paper baking cups in a muffin pan. In a large bowl, combine all the cupcake ingredients. Beat on a low speed with an electric mixer until all the ingredients are combined. Spoon the mixture into the cups. Bake for 20 minutes. Remove pan from the oven and cool for 5 minutes. Remove the cupcakes and cool on a rack. To make the frosting, combine the cream cheese with the confectioners' sugar and vanilla with an electric mixer. Beat until smooth and creamy. Fold in the walnuts. Smear onto the cooled cupcakes and garnish with the walnut halves.

Store unfrosted in an airtight container for up to 3 days, or freeze for up to 3 months.

Makes 1 dozen

ultimate flourless choc cupcakes

see variations page 245

For maximum luxury, top with chocolate cream.

for the cupcakes
1 1/2 cups bittersweet chocolate chips
1 cup (2 sticks) sweet butter
4 large eggs
4 large egg yolks
1/2 cup granulated sugar
2 tbsp. Dutch-process cocoa powder, sifted
2 tbsp. ground almonds
1 tsp. vanilla extract

for the frosting
2 tbsp. Dutch-process cocoa powder
4 tbsp. confectioners' sugar
1 1/2 cups heavy cream
1 tsp. vanilla extract
1/2 tsp. orange extract

Preheat the oven to 375°F (190°C). Place 12 paper baking cups in a muffin pan. Put the chocolate and butter in a double boiler, or medium bowl over a pan of simmering water, and stir until completely melted. Set aside to cool. In a large bowl, cream the eggs, yolks, and sugar with an electric mixer until pale and thick. Gently fold in the melted chocolate and remaining ingredients. Spoon the batter into the cups. Bake for 20 minutes. Remove pan from the oven and cool for 5 minutes. Then remove the cupcakes and cool on a rack.

To make the frosting, sift the cocoa and confectioners' sugar together into a medium bowl. Add the cream, vanilla, and orange extract. Beat until soft, but the cream should still hold its shape. Spoon over the warm cupcakes.

Makes 1 dozen

chocolate vegan cupcakes

see variations page 246

To make this authentically vegan, you must use specially labeled vegan chocolate chips.

2 1/2 cups all-purpose flour
4 tbsp. Dutch-process cocoa powder
Pinch of salt
2 cups granulated sugar
1/2 cup unsweetened applesauce
2 cups cold water
2 tsp. white vinegar
2 tsp. baking soda
1 cup semisweet vegan chocolate chips
Cocoa powder for dusting

Preheat the oven to 375°F (190°C). Place 12 paper baking cups in a muffin pan. Sift the flour, cocoa, salt, and sugar into a large bowl and set aside.

In a separate large bowl, combine the applesauce, water, vinegar, and baking soda. Add the flour mixture and stir well to combine. Fold in the chocolate chips.

Spoon the mixture into the cups. Bake for about 20 minutes.

Remove pan from the oven and cool for 5 minutes. Then remove the cupcakes and cool on a rack. Serve dusted with cocoa. Store in an airtight container for up to 3 days, or freeze for up to 3 months.

Makes 1 dozen

g.i. carrot cupcakes

see variations page 247

These cupcakes are perfect for those using the glycemic index to monitor their diet. Low glycemic foods release their sugars slowly — and are thus more beneficial for maintaining blood sugar levels.

1/2 cup light vegetable oil
1/2 cup packed brown sugar
1 large egg, lightly beaten
3 large egg whites
1 cup shredded carrots
1 cup shredded Granny Smith apples
1 cup raisins

1/2 cup chopped dates
1/2 cup mixed dried berries
1/2 cup chopped walnuts
1 tsp. allspice
1 tsp. baking powder
1 tsp. salt
2 3/4 cups whole wheat pastry flour

Preheat the oven to 350°F (175°C). Place 12 paper baking cups into a muffin pan. In a large bowl, combine the oil and sugar, and beat with an electric mixer until light and smooth, about 2 to 3 minutes. Beat the egg and egg whites, one at a time, and then add the carrots, apples, dried fruits, and walnuts. Sift the rest of the ingredients into a medium mixing bowl. Add them to the carrot mixture, stirring until just combined. Spoon the mixture into the cups. Bake for 20 minutes. Remove pan from the oven and cool for 5 minutes. Then remove the cupcakes and cool on a rack. Serve with a low-fat margarine spread.

Store in an airtight container for up to 3 days, or freeze for up to 3 months.

Makes 1 dozen

dairy-free berry cupcakes

see variations page 248

These little treats are wonderful for the lactose-intolerant cupcake lover.

for the cupcakes
2 1/2 cups mixed fresh berries (blueberries,
    strawberries, cranberries, blackberries)
2 cups all-purpose flour
1/2 cup packed brown sugar
1 tbsp. baking powder

4 tbsp. vegetable oil
2 large eggs, lightly beaten

for the topping
1/2 cup mixed berry jam

Preheat the oven to 350°F (175°C). Place 12 paper baking cups into a muffin pan. In a food processor, purée 1 1/2 cups of the berries until smooth. In a small bowl, lightly crush the reserved berries with a fork. In a medium bowl, mix the flour, sugar, and baking powder. In a large bowl, beat the oil and eggs. Add the puréed berries and mix well. Stir in the flour mixture until combined. Fold in the crushed berries.

Spoon the batter into the cups. Top each cupcake with a teaspoon of jam. Bake for 20 minutes. Remove pan from the oven and cool for 5 minutes. Then remove the cupcakes and cool on a rack.

Store in an airtight container for up to 3 days, or freeze for up to 3 months.

Makes 1 dozen

gluten-free pecan cupcakes

see variations page 249

Gluten-free flour has a variety of uses. Look for it in specialty food or health stores. Add a little more liquid than you would when using normal flour, since it will be absorbed.

2 3/4 cups gluten-free all-purpose flour
3/4 cup granulated sugar
1 1/2 tbsp. baking powder
Pinch of salt
2 large eggs, lightly beaten
4 tbsp. sweet butter, melted
1 1/4 cups milk
1 tsp. vanilla extract
1 cup roughly chopped pecans
1/2 cup chopped dates

Preheat the oven to 400°F (200°C). Grease a 12-cup muffin pan.

In a medium bowl, mix the flour, sugar, baking powder, and salt. In a large bowl, beat the eggs, butter, milk, and vanilla. Add the dry ingredients and stir until nearly combined. Fold in the pecans and dates.

Spoon the mixture into the prepared pan. Bake for 20 minutes. Remove pan from the oven and cool for 5 minutes. Then remove the muffins and cool on a rack.

Store in an airtight container for up to 3 days, or freeze for up to 3 months.

Makes 1 dozen

mini couscous cupcakes

see base recipe page 209

mini couscous & cilantro cakes
Prepare the basic cupcake recipe, adding 2 tablespoons freshly chopped cilantro along with the lemon zest and parsley.

mini couscous cakes with preserved lemon & thyme
Prepare the basic cupcake recipe, adding 1 teaspoon chopped preserved lemon and 1 tablespoon chopped thyme leaves along with the lemon zest and parsley.

mini couscous cakes with olive & chile
Prepare the basic cupcake recipe, adding 3 tablespoons tapenade or olive paste and 1 teaspoon chopped chile pepper along with the lemon zest and parsley.

mini couscous cakes with chipotle
Prepare the basic cupcake recipe, adding 2 tablespoons finely chopped canned chipotle in adobo, and substituting lime for lemon zest and chopped cilantro for parsley.

variations

basil pesto cupcakes

see base recipe page 210

basil pesto & cilantro cupcakes
Prepare the basic cupcake recipe, adding 3 tablespoons finely chopped cilantro to the frosting.

red pepper pesto cupcakes
Prepare the basic cupcake recipe, substituting 1/2 cup (3 oz.) red pepper pesto for the basil pesto.

basil pesto & chili cupcakes
Prepare the basic cupcake recipe, adding 1 teaspoon chili flakes to the batter before it has been mixed together.

horseradish & bacon cupcakes
Prepare the basic cupcake recipe, adding 2 strips crisply cooked and chopped bacon to the batter before it has been mixed together. For the frosting, substitute 2 teaspoons prepared horseradish for the pesto and 1 cup (2 oz.) chopped scallions for the tomatoes.

southwest-style cornbread cupcakes
Prepare the basic cupcake recipe, adding 1 small chopped jalapeño pepper to the batter before it has been mixed together. For the frosting, substitute salsa for the pesto and 1/2 cup (8 tbsp.) chopped cilantro for the tomatoes.

variations

pb & banana cupcakes

see base recipe page 212

banana & pecan cupcakes
Prepare the basic cupcake recipe, substituting 4 tablespoons of chopped pecans for the peanut butter chips.

pb & banana cupcakes with maple syrup & ginger frosting
Prepare the basic cupcake recipe. Stir in 3 tablespoons chopped candied ginger along with the peanut butter chips and mashed banana. In the frosting, substitute 4 tablespoons maple syrup for the confectioners' sugar.

pb, banana & chocolate chip cupcakes
Prepare the basic cupcake recipe, adding 4 tablespoons of semisweet chocolate chips after creaming the batter.

pb, banana & blueberry cupcakes
Prepare the basic cupcake recipe, adding 4 tablespoons of dried blueberries after creaming the batter.

pb & pumpkin cupcakes
Prepare the basic cupcake recipe, substituting 1 cup (6 oz.) canned pumpkin for the banana.

variations

ricotta cheesecake cupcakes

see base recipe page 215

banana & raisin ricotta cheesecake cupcakes
Prepare the basic recipe but use only 3 cups (1 lb 8 oz.) ricotta cheese. Add
3/4 cup (about 2 medium) mashed bananas to the ricotta cheese after
adding the eggs and confectioners' sugar. Add 1/2 cup (3 1/2 oz.) raisins.

blueberry ricotta cheesecake cupcakes
Prepare the basic cheesecake mixture, folding in 1 cup (4 1/2 oz.)
fresh blueberries.

raspberry & lime ricotta cheesecake cupcakes
Prepare the basic cheesecake mixture, folding in 1 cup (5 oz.) fresh
raspberries and 1 tablespoon freshly grated lime zest.

pumpkin cheesecake cupcakes
Prepare the basic recipe but use only 3 cups (1 lb 8 oz.) ricotta cheese. Add
3/4 cup (5 oz.) canned pumpkin pie filling to the ricotta cheese after adding
the eggs and confectioners' sugar. Omit the orange extract and the walnuts.

variations

low-fat vanilla cupcakes

see base recipe page 216

low-fat cupcakes with fennel & orange drizzle
Prepare the basic cupcake mixture. In the glaze, substitute 2 teaspoons
lightly crushed fennel seeds for the poppy seeds, and substitute
1 teaspoon orange extract for the vanilla extract.

low-fat cupcakes with strawberry & lime drizzle
Prepare the basic cupcake mixture. In the glaze, substitute 1 teaspoon
strawberry extract for the vanilla, and add 1 tablespoon freshly grated
lime zest to the mixture.

low-fat cupcakes with almond & cherry drizzle
Prepare the basic cupcake mixture. In the glaze, substitute 1 teaspoon
almond extract for the vanilla extract. Add 2 tablespoons chopped
candied cherries.

low-fat cappuccino cupcakes
Prepare the basic cupcake mixture, adding 1 teaspoon cinnamon. In the
glaze, substitute freshly brewed dark coffee for the lemon juice. Omit the
poppy seeds. Decorate with chocolate sprinkles.

flour-lite chocolate cupcakes

see base recipe page 217

flour-lite chocolate & orange cupcakes
Prepare the basic cupcake recipe, substituting 2 teaspoons orange extract for the vanilla extract.

flour-lite chocolate-glazed cupcakes
Prepare the basic cupcake recipe. Make a glaze: Sift 1 1/2 cups (7 1/2 oz.) confectioners' sugar and 2 tablespoons Dutch-process cocoa powder into a medium bowl. Beat 2 tablespoons softened margarine into the cocoa powder mixture, adding 1 tablespoon warm water and 1 tablespoon coffee liqueur to make a pourable consistency. Spoon over the cupcakes.

flour-lite chocolate & cinnamon cupcakes
Prepare the basic cupcake recipe, adding 2 teaspoons cinnamon to the dry ingredients.

flour-lite chocolate & chile cupcakes
Prepare the basic cupcake recipe, adding 2 teaspoons ground ancho chile to the dry ingredients.

quick applesauce cupcakes

see base recipe page 218

quick applesauce & pecan cupcakes
Prepare the basic cupcake recipe, adding 3 tablespoons chopped pecans
after adding the dry ingredients. For the topping, substitute 3 tablespoons
chopped pecans for the walnuts.

quick applesauce & raisin cupcakes
Prepare the basic cupcake recipe, adding 4 tablespoons raisins after adding
the dry ingredients.

quick applesauce & cranberry cupcakes
Prepare the basic cupcake recipe, adding 4 tablespoons dried cranberries
after adding the dry ingredients.

quick applesauce & black walnut cupcakes
Prepare the basic cupcake recipe, adding 3 tablespoons chopped black
walnuts after adding the dry ingredients. For the topping, substitute
3 tablespoons chopped black walnuts for the walnuts.

glazed blueberry–lime cupcakes

see base recipe page 219

glazed raspberry–lemon cupcakes
Prepare the basic cupcake recipe, substituting 1 cup (4 1/2 oz.) fresh raspberries for the blueberries, and 1 tablespoon grated lemon zest for the lime zest in the glaze.

glazed blackberry–orange cupcakes
Prepare the basic cupcake recipe, substituting 1 cup (4 1/2 oz.) fresh blackberries for the blueberries, and 1 tablespoon grated orange zest for the lime zest in the glaze.

glazed strawberry–lime cupcakes
Prepare the basic cupcake recipe, substituting 1 cup (4 1/2 oz.) fresh sliced strawberries for the blueberries.

glazed coconut–lime cupcakes
Prepare the basic cupcake recipe, substituting 1 cup (2 1/2 oz.) sweetened, flaked coconut for the blueberries.

banana & honey cupcakes

see base recipe page 221

banana, hazelnut & honey cupcakes
Prepare the basic cupcake recipe, substituting 3/4 cup (5 oz.) roughly chopped unblanched hazelnuts for the walnuts.

banana & maple syrup cupcakes
Prepare the basic cupcake recipe, substituting 1/4 cup (2 fl. oz.) maple syrup for the honey.

banana, pecan & corn syrup cupcakes
Prepare the basic cupcake recipe, substituting 3/4 cup (5 oz.) roughly chopped pecans for the walnuts, and 1/4 cup (2 fl. oz.) corn syrup for the honey.

banana, honey & blueberry cupcakes
Prepare the basic cupcake recipe, substituting 3/4 cup (5 oz.) dried blueberries for the walnuts.

marbled mini bundt cakes

see base recipe page 222

marbled mini raisin bundt cakes
Prepare the basic cupcake recipe. After dividing the batters, add 3 tablespoons golden raisins to the plain batter.

marbled mini orange & walnut bundt cakes
Prepare the basic cupcake recipe. After dividing the batters, add 1 teaspoon orange extract to the chocolate batter, and 3 tablespoons chopped walnuts to the plain batter.

marbled mini pistachio bundt cakes
Prepare the basic cupcake recipe. After dividing the batters, add 3 tablespoons chopped pistachio nuts to the plain batter.

marbled mini chocolate orange bundt cakes
Prepare the basic cupcake recipe. After dividing the batters, add 1 teaspoon orange extract to the chocolate batter, and 3 tablespoons chopped candied orange to the plain batter.

low-fat carrot & nut cupcakes

see base recipe page 224

low-fat carrot & pecan cupcakes
Prepare the basic cupcake mixture, substituting 1/2 cup (3 1/2 oz.) of roughly chopped pecans for the walnuts. Substitute 4 tablespoons chopped pecans for the walnuts in the frosting, and substitute 12 pecans for the walnut halves for garnishing.

low-fat ginger-frosted carrot cupcakes
Prepare the basic cupcake mixture. In the frosting, substitute 3 tablespoons chopped candied ginger for the chopped walnuts.

low-fat carrot & orange cupcakes
Prepare the basic cupcake mixture, adding 1 teaspoon orange extract and 1 teaspoon ground cumin to the cupcakes.

low-fat carrot, zucchini & yellow squash cupcakes
Prepare the basic cupcake mixture, substituting 2 tablespoons grated zucchini and 2 tablespoons grated yellow squash for 1/4 cup (1 oz.) of the carrots.

ultimate flourless choc cupcakes

see base recipe page 226

ultimate flourless peppermint cream cupcakes
Prepare the basic cupcake recipe. Substitute 1 teaspoon peppermint extract
for the vanilla and orange extract.

ultimate flourless vanilla ice cream cupcakes
Prepare the basic cupcake recipe. Make an ice cream topping: Mix 2 cups
(12 oz.) ready-made pudding and 1 1/4 cups (10 fl. oz.) heavy cream in a
large bowl, and beat well. Add 1 teaspoon vanilla extract. Pour into an ice
cream maker and churn until frozen. Put 1 scoop on top of each cupcake.

ultimate flourless strawberry cream cupcakes
Prepare the basic cupcake recipe. In the frosting, substitute 1 teaspoon
strawberry extract for the vanilla extract. Fold in 1/2 cup (2 oz.) finely
chopped fresh strawberries after beating the cream.

ultimate flourless coffee cream cupcakes
Prepare the basic cupcake recipe. Substitute 1 teaspoon coffee extract for
the vanilla and orange extract.

variations

chocolate vegan cupcakes

see base recipe page 227

chocolate & orange vegan cupcakes
Prepare the basic cupcake recipe, adding 1 1/2 tablespoons grated orange zest to the mixture along with the chocolate chips.

chocolate & hazelnut vegan cupcakes
Prepare the basic cupcake recipe, adding 1/2 cup (3 1/2 oz.) chopped roasted hazelnuts along with the chocolate chips.

chocolate & coffee vegan cupcakes
Prepare the basic cupcake recipe, adding 1/4 cup (2 fl. oz.) hot coffee to the applesauce mixture.

chocolate & ginger vegan cupcakes
Prepare the basic cupcake recipe, adding 2 tablespoons grated fresh ginger to the applesauce mixture.

g.i. carrot cupcakes

see base recipe page 228

g.i. pecan cupcakes
Prepare the basic cupcake mixture, substituting 1/2 cup (3 1/2 oz.) chopped pecans for the walnuts.

g.i. banana cupcakes
Prepare the basic cupcake mixture, adding 1/2 cup (about 1 1/2 bananas) mashed bananas along with the carrots and fruits. Substitute 1/2 teaspoon nutmeg for the allspice.

g.i. currant cupcakes
Prepare the basic cupcake mixture, substituting 1 cup (7 oz.) currants for the raisins.

g.i. apricot almond cupcakes
Prepare the basic cupcake mixture, substituting 1 cup (7 oz.) snipped dried apricots for the raisins and 1/2 cup (2 oz.) chopped almonds for the walnuts.

variations

dairy-free berry cupcakes

see base recipe page 230

dairy-free apple & berry cupcakes
Prepare the basic cupcake recipe, substituting 1 1/2 cups (6 oz.) unsweetened applesauce for 1 1/2 cups (6 oz.) of the mixed berries.

dairy-free pear & berry cupcakes
Prepare the basic cupcake recipe, substituting 1 1/2 cups (9 oz.) puréed canned pears for 1 1/2 cups (6 oz.) of the mixed berries. Add 1 teaspoon almond extract to the batter.

dairy-free peach & berry cupcakes
Prepare the basic cupcake recipe, substituting 1 1/2 cups (9 oz.) puréed canned peaches for 1 1/2 cups of the mixed berries.

dairy-free apricot cupcakes
Prepare the basic cupcake recipe, substituting 2 1/2 cups (8 oz.) chopped, canned apricots for the mixed berries. For the topping, substitute 1/2 cup (6 oz.) apricot preserves for the berry jam.

gluten–free pecan cupcakes

see base recipe page 232

gluten-free mixed peel cupcakes
Prepare the basic cupcake recipe, substituting 1/2 cup (3 1/2 oz.) chopped candied mixed peel for the dates.

gluten-free apricot cupcakes
Prepare the basic cupcake recipe, substituting 1/2 cup (3 1/2 oz.) chopped dried apricots for the dates.

gluten-free molasses cupcakes
Prepare the basic cupcake recipe, omitting the sugar and adding 4 tablespoons molasses and 4 tablespoons of honey to the milk mixture.

gluten-free sorghum cupcakes
Prepare the basic cupcake recipe, omitting the sugar and adding 1/2 cup (2 1/2 oz.) of sorghum to the milk mixture.

designer cupcakes

A few artful twists can take cupcakes to a new, fun
level. Designer Buttercream Frosting, Moldable
White Chocolate, cookies, and candies make
decorating easy.

designer buttercream

This light and fluffy frosting can be flavored and tinted any way you wish, and will keep, covered, in the refrigerator for a week, or frozen for several months.

1 cup (2 sticks) unsalted butter, softened
1/2 cup vegetable shortening
4 large egg whites
2 tsp. lemon juice

1/2 teaspoon cream of tartar
1/2 cup granulated sugar
1/4 cup water
2 tsp. vanilla extract

Beat the butter and shortening together in a food processor until smooth; set aside in a cool area.

Using a stand mixer, whip the egg whites with the lemon juice, and cream of tartar until soft peaks form; set aside. Stir the sugar and water together in a saucepan until the sugar has dissolved. Cook over medium-high heat until a candy thermometer inserted in the syrup registers 250°F, about 10 minutes.

Pour the hot syrup in a thin stream into the beaten egg whites, beating constantly at low speed, until you have a thick, glossy frosting. Beat in the vanilla. Continue beating on medium speed until the bottom of bowl is as warm as your face, about 98°F. Set aside to cool for 5 minutes.

Switch to the paddle attachment and add the butter mixture, 2 tablespoons at a time, beating well after each addition until smooth and creamy. If the frosting breaks, continue beating at low to medium speed and the mixture will come back together. Cool for about an hour before using.

day at the beach

see variations page 272

Roll out the striped towel, open the parasol, and enjoy the waves lapping at the beach—
all in miniature on top of the cupcake.

1 cup (2 sticks) sweet butter, softened
1 cup granulated sugar
2 cups cake flour
2 tsp. baking powder
1 tsp. salt
4 large eggs
1/2 cup buttermilk
1 1/2 tsp. vanilla extract

for the frosting & decorations
1 recipe Designer Buttercream (page 251)
few drops of food coloring
2 cups graham cracker crumbs
18 party drink parasols
18 sticks fruit-striped candy, cut into 2-inch
  pieces

Preheat the oven to 350°F (175°C). Place 18 paper baking cups in muffin pans.

Place all the ingredients in a medium bowl and beat with an electric mixer until smooth
and pale, about 2 to 3 minutes. Spoon the mixture into the cups. Bake for 20 minutes or
until a cake tester inserted in the center comes out clean. Remove the pans from the oven
and cool for 5 minutes. Then remove the cupcakes and cool on a rack.

Leave 2/3 of the frosting white. Tint the other 1/3 ocean blue. For each cupcake: Frost
2/3 of the top with white frosting and sprinkle with graham cracker crumbs for the beach.
Frost the other 1/3 with blue frosting, creating "waves" with a knife. Lay the candy on the
diagonal across the "sand" for a beach towel and insert the parasol at an angle to make the
beach umbrella.

Makes 1 1/2 dozen

daisy daze

see variations page 273

Snipped-on-the-diagonal miniature marshmallows, cut sides dipped in colored sugar, form the petals on these flowery cupcakes.

1 cup (2 sticks) sweet butter, softened
1 cup granulated sugar
2 cups cake flour
2 tsp. baking powder
1 tsp. salt
4 large eggs
1/2 cup buttermilk
1 1/2 tsp. vanilla extract

for the frosting & decorations
1 recipe Designer Buttercream (page 251)
Yellow food coloring
4 cups miniature marshmallows
18 lemon gumdrops, lemon balls, or other small, circular lemon candies
Yellow decorating sugar

Preheat the oven to 350°F (175°C). Place 18 paper baking cups in muffin pans. Place all the ingredients in a medium bowl and beat with an electric mixer until smooth and pale, about 2 to 3 minutes. Spoon the mixture into the cups. Bake for 20 minutes or until a cake tester inserted in the center comes out clean.

Remove the pans from the oven and cool for 5 minutes. Then remove the cupcakes and cool on a rack.

Tint the frosting yellow. For each cupcake: Frost the top. Place a lemon gumdrop in the center. Snip each miniature marshmallow in half lengthwise, press cut side in yellow sugar, and arrange sugared side up around the gumdrop like petals.

Makes 1 1/2 dozen

clown

see variations page 274

These colorful cupcakes could be a big hit at a children's party. Choose sugar cones with a pointed end.

1 cup (2 sticks) sweet butter, softened
1 cup granulated sugar
2 cups cake flour
2 tsp. baking powder
1 tsp. salt
4 large eggs
1/2 cup buttermilk
1 1/2 tsp. vanilla extract

for the frosting & decorations
1 recipe Designer Buttercream (page 251)
2 lbs. white chocolate chips
18 sugar cones with pointed ends
Colored sprinkles
1 recipe Moldable White Chocolate (page 15)
Red food coloring

Preheat the oven to 350°F (175°C). Place 18 paper baking cups in muffin pans. Place all the ingredients in a medium bowl and beat with an electric mixer until smooth and pale, about 2 to 3 minutes. Spoon the mixture into the cups. Bake for 20 minutes or until a cake tester inserted in the center comes out clean. Remove the pans from the oven and cool for 5 minutes. Then remove the cupcakes and cool on a rack. Keep the frosting white. For each cupcake: Frost the top. Melt the white chocolate chips. Lightly brush it over the outside of each sugar cone and roll in colored sprinkles. Let set. Tint Moldable White Chocolate red, divide it into 18 pieces. Pinch off a small portion from each piece and roll into a ball. Roll the rest of the piece into a 16-inch-long rope on a confectioners' sugar-dusted surface. Place the sugar cone firmly in the center of each cupcake and secure the red ball on the pointed end. Loop the rope around the circumference of the cone to make clown hair. Scatter more colored sprinkles on the frosting.

Makes 1 1/2 dozen

spider web

see variations page 275

Inject a little mystery into your cupcake art.

1 cup (2 sticks) sweet butter, softened
1 cup granulated sugar
2 cups cake flour
2 tsp. baking powder
1 tsp. salt
4 large eggs
1/2 cup buttermilk
1 1/2 tsp. vanilla extract

for the frosting & decorations
1 recipe Designer Buttercream (page 251)
Black gel icing
18 licorice gumdrops
18 black craft pipe cleaners or chenille sticks

Preheat the oven to 350°F (175°C). Place 18 paper baking cups in muffin pans. Place all the ingredients in a medium bowl and beat with an electric mixer until smooth and pale, about 2 to 3 minutes. Spoon the mixture into the cups. Bake for 20 minutes or until a cake tester inserted in the center comes out clean.

Remove the pans from the oven and cool for 5 minutes. Then remove the cupcakes and cool on a rack.

Keep the frosting white. For each cupcake: Frost the top. Using a black gel icing tube, draw three concentric circles radiating out from the center of the cupcake. With a knife, draw across the frosting and icing in four places to create the spider web. Place a large licorice gumdrop in the center of the cupcake. Cut each pipe cleaner into 8 pieces and fold in half to create legs. Arrange the legs around the gumdrop.

Makes 1 1/2 dozen

how does your garden grow?

see variations page 276

Even if you don't have a green thumb, you can still have a garden atop a cupcake.

1 cup (2 sticks) sweet butter, softened
1 cup granulated sugar
2 cups cake flour
1 tsp. baking powder
1/2 tsp. salt
4 large eggs
1/2 cup buttermilk
1 tsp. vanilla extract
for the frosting & decorations
3 1/2 oz. semisweet chocolate, roughly chopped

2 tbsp. milk
1/4 cup (1/2 stick) sweet butter
3/4 cup confectioners' sugar, sifted
2 1/2 cups crushed chocolate sandwich cookies
2 1/2 cups sweetened flaked coconut
    tinted green
12 oz. ready-to-roll white fondant frosting
Brown, orange, and green food coloring
Sugar pearls to decorate
18 toothpicks

Preheat the oven to 350°F (175°C). Place 18 paper baking cups into muffin pans. Combine all the cupcake ingredients in a medium bowl and beat with an electric mixer until smooth and pale, about 2 to 3 minutes. Spoon the batter into the cups. Bake for 20 minutes. Remove the pans from the oven and cool for 5 minutes. Remove the cupcakes and cool on the rack. To make the frosting, gently heat the chocolate, milk, and butter in a small, heavy saucepan, stirring until melted. Remove from the heat and beat in the confectioners' sugar. Frost the top of each cupcake, and sprinkle with cookie crumbs. Arrange two parallel rows of green coconut. Split the fondant frosting into thirds, and tint each a different color. Shape carrots from orange and green fondant frosting. Shape cauliflowers from green fondant frosting, decorate with sugar pearls, and arrange on top of each cupcake. Shape a shovel from brown frosting — use a toothpick to support the shaft, and position the shovel on each cupcake.

Makes 1 1/2 dozen

bride doll

see variations page 277

For a little girl's birthday party or a bridal shower, these doll cupcakes can be customized with frosting colors and decorations. Mini dolls on picks are available at craft stores and cake decorating shops.

1 cup (2 sticks) sweet butter, softened
1 cup granulated sugar
2 cups cake flour
2 tsp. baking powder
1 tsp. salt
4 large eggs
1/2 cup buttermilk
1 1/2 tsp. vanilla extract

for the frosting & decorations
1 double recipe Designer Buttercream
  (page 251)
18 (4 1/4-inch) mini dolls on picks
Sugar pearls
White sugar flowers

Preheat the oven to 350°F (175°C). Place 18 paper baking cups in muffin pans. Place all the ingredients in a medium bowl and beat with an electric mixer until smooth and pale, about 2 to 3 minutes. Spoon the mixture into the cups. Bake for 20 minutes or until a cake tester inserted in the center comes out clean. Remove the pans from the oven and cool for 5 minutes. Then remove the cupcakes and cool on a rack. When cool, remove the cupcake wrappers and turn the cupcakes upside down. Reserve 1/3 of the frosting.

For each cupcake: Frost the top and sides of cupcake. Insert a doll in the center. Spoon the reserved frosting into a piping bag or a sealable plastic bag with an end corner snipped and pipe the frosting to form a strapless bodice on each doll. Create a pattern on each dress using sugar pearls and flowers.

Makes 1 1/2 dozen

ruffles & pearls

see variations page 278

Roll out, roll up, and form stunning fondant roses to top each cupcake for an elegant finish.

1 cup (2 sticks) sweet butter, softened
1 cup granulated sugar
2 cups cake flour
2 tsp. baking powder
1 tsp. salt
4 large eggs
1/2 cup buttermilk
1 1/2 tsp. vanilla extract

for the frosting & decorations
1 recipe Designer Buttercream (page 251)
1 recipe Moldable White Chocolate (page 15)
Confectioners' sugar
White sugar pearls

Preheat the oven to 350°F (175°C). Place 18 paper baking cups in muffin pans. Place all the ingredients in a medium bowl and beat with an electric mixer until smooth and pale, about 2 to 3 minutes. Spoon the mixture into the cups. Bake for 20 minutes or until a cake tester inserted in the center comes out clean. Remove the pans from the oven and cool for 5 minutes. Then remove the cupcakes and cool on a rack.

Leave the frosting white. Divide the Moldable White Chocolate into 9 pieces. On a flat surface heavily dusted with confectioners' sugar, dust each piece with the sugar and roll out to a 16-inch oval. Starting at a long end and using a metal spatula, roll it up. Cut the roll in half in the middle to form 2 (2 1/2-inch) ruffled pieces. For each cupcake: Frost the top with white frosting. Place the cut side of a ruffled piece in the center and gently spread the ruffles. Sprinkle with sugar pearls.

Makes 1 1/2 dozen

morning latte

see variations page 279

The morning cup of java just got a little sweeter — and more interesting! Coordinate the color of the pipe cleaner "handles" with the colors of your cupcake paper liners.

for the cupcakes
1 cup (2 sticks) sweet butter, softened
1 cup granulated sugar
2 cups cake flour
1 tsp. baking powder
1/2 tsp. salt
4 large eggs
1 tsp. vanilla extract

for the frosting
3 1/2 oz. semisweet chocolate, roughly chopped
2 tbsp. freshly brewed dark coffee
1/4 cup (1/2 stick) sweet butter
3/4 cup confectioners' sugar, sifted

for the decorations
1 (7 1/2 oz.) jar Marshmallow Fluff or 4 cups
    miniature marshmallows, melted
18 craft pipe cleaners or chenille sticks

Preheat the oven to 350°F (175°C). Place 18 paper baking cups into muffin pans. Combine all the cupcake ingredients in a medium bowl and beat with an electric mixer until smooth and pale, about 2 to 3 minutes. Spoon the batter into the cups. Bake for 20 minutes. Remove the pans from the oven and cool for 5 minutes. Remove the cupcakes and cool on a rack.

To make the frosting, gently heat the chocolate, coffee, and butter in a small, heavy saucepan, stirring until melted. Remove from the heat and beat in the confectioners' sugar. For each cupcake: Frost the top. Pipe or spoon marshmallow fluff on top of each cupcake. Bend the pipe cleaner into a U-shape and insert both ends into the side of each cupcake wrapper to form a "handle."

Makes 1 1/2 dozen

aquarium

see variations page 280

You don't have to leave home to visit the aquarium!

1 cup (2 sticks) sweet butter, softened
1 cup granulated sugar
2 cups cake flour
2 tsp. baking powder
1 tsp. salt
4 large eggs
1/2 cup buttermilk
1 1/2 tsp. vanilla extract

for the frosting & decorations
1 recipe Designer Buttercream (page 251)
Blue food coloring
60 assorted Swedish gummy fish, or other
    gummy sea creature shapes
Candy rocks or crushed nut cookies

Preheat the oven to 350°F (175°C). Place 18 paper baking cups in muffin pans. Place all the cupcake ingredients in a medium bowl and beat with an electric mixer until smooth and pale, about 2 to 3 minutes. Spoon the mixture into the cups. Bake for 20 minutes or until a cake tester inserted in the center comes out clean.

Remove the pans from the oven and cool for 5 minutes. Remove the cupcakes and cool on a rack.

When the cupcakes have cooled, tint the frosting sea blue. For each cupcake: Frost the top. Use a knife to make "waves" on the top third of the cupcake. Place candy fish and sea creatures among the waves. Scatter candy rocks on the lower third of the cupcake to form the aquarium bed.

Makes 1 1/2 dozen

garden hat

see variations page 281

Yellow cake, colored frosting, fruit-striped gummy candy as bonnet trim, sugar pearls or candy flowers. Stacked vanilla wafers, frosted over, form the peak of the hat.

1 cup (2 sticks) sweet butter, softened
1 cup granulated sugar
2 cups cake flour
2 tsp. baking powder
1 tsp. salt
4 large eggs
1/2 cup buttermilk
1 1/2 tsp. vanilla extract

for the frosting & decorations
1 recipe Designer Buttercream (page 251)
Yellow food coloring
36 vanilla wafers
9 sticks fruit-striped gummy candy
Colored candy balls and flowers

Preheat the oven to 350°F (175°C). Place 18 paper baking cups in muffin pans. Place all the ingredients in a medium bowl and beat with an electric mixer until smooth and pale, about 2 to 3 minutes. Spoon the mixture into the cups. Bake for 20 minutes or until a cake tester inserted in the center comes out clean.

Remove the pans from the oven and cool for 5 minutes. Remove the cupcakes and cool on a rack.

When the cupcakes have cooled, tint the frosting yellow. For each cupcake: Frost the top. Sandwich two vanilla wafers together with frosting and place in the center of the cupcake. Frost over that. Cut a stick of candy in half lengthwise and form a band around the stacked wafers, notching the end. Decorate around the hat band with colored candy balls and flowers.

Makes 1 1/2 dozen

variations

day at the beach

see base recipe page 252

day on the lake
Prepare the basic cupcake recipe. Omit beach parasols and cookie crumbs.
Tint all frosting blue. For each cupcake: Frost the top, creating waves with a
knife. Place 3 small Swedish candy fish among the waves. Thread a 2-inch
piece of fruit stripe candy through a colored toothpick to make a sail and
insert toothpick in center of a thick orange fruit slice candy. Place "sailboat"
in center of each cupcake.

day on the ski slope
Prepare the basic cupcake recipe. Omit beach parasols and cookie crumbs.
Keep frosting white. For each cupcake: Frost the top, mounding frosting up
on one side to create a ski slope and dust with crystal sanding sugar. Tint
Moldable White Chocolate (page 15) dark green, divide it into 18 pieces, and
cut each piece into 6 portions. Mold each portion into a 1-inch cone and
snip randomly and diagonally around the cone with kitchen shears. Gently
lift out snipped areas to form evergreen branches. Place 3 evergreen trees
flanking each side of the ski slope. Place a tiny plastic skier on
the slope.

daisy daze

see base recipe page 255

black-eyed susan

Prepare the basic cupcake recipe. Substitute a combination of yellow and orange decorating sugars for yellow. Substitute semisweet chocolate chips for lemon candies. For each cupcake: frost the top. Place three semisweet chocolate chips in the center. Snip each miniature marshmallow in half on the diagonal, dip on cut side in yellow-orange sugar, and arrange sugared side up around the center like rows of petals.

dahlia

Prepare the basic cupcake recipe. Substitute a combination of red and orange decorating sugars for yellow. Substitute orange gumdrops for lemon candies. For each cupcake: frost the top. Place an orange gumdrop in the center. Snip each miniature marshmallow in half on the diagonal, dip cut side in a mixture of orange and red sugar, and arrange sugared side up around the gumdrop like rows of petals.

zinnia

Prepare the basic cupcake recipe. Substitute a combination of red and pink decorating sugars for yellow. Substitute yellow gumdrops for lemon candies. For each cupcake: frost the top. Place a yellow gumdrop in the center. Snip each miniature marshmallow in half on the diagonal, dip on cut side in a mixture of pink and red sanding sugars, and arrange sugared side up around the gumdrop like rows of petals.

clown

see base recipe page 257

princess

Prepare the basic cupcake recipe. Tint the melted white chocolate light pink, brush on the cones, and roll in pink and white sprinkles. Tint Moldable White Chocolate pink, divide it into 18 pieces. Pinch off a small portion from each piece and roll into a ball. Roll the rest of the piece into a 16-inch-long rope. Place the sugar cone firmly in the center of each cupcake and secure the pink ball on the pointed end. Loop the rope around the circumference of the cone to make ruffled edge. Scatter more sprinkles on the frosting.

christmas tree

Prepare the basic cupcake recipe. Tint the melted white chocolate green, brush on the cones, and roll in colored sprinkles. Tint Moldable White Chocolate yellow, divide it into 18 pieces. Pinch off a small portion from each piece and form it into a star. Roll the rest of the piece into a 16-inch-long rope. Place the sugar cone firmly in the center of each cupcake and secure the star on the pointed end. Loop the rope around the circumference of the cone to make a tree skirt. Scatter more colored sprinkles on the frosting.

variations

spider web

see base recipe page 259

soccer ball
Prepare the basic cupcake recipe. Keep the frosting white. For each cupcake, frost the top. Using a black gel icing tube, draw a hexagon in the center of the cupcake. Draw a line from the six corners or points of the hexagon out to the edge of the cupcake. Omit gumdrops and pipe cleaners.

campfire
Prepare the basic cupcake recipe. Tint the frosting green. For each cupcake, frost the top, but omit basic decorations. Cut thin chocolate-covered tube-shaped cookies or chocolates into 2-inch "logs" and stack in the center of the cupcake. Cut orange or yellow fruit-striped candy into "flames" and place amidst the logs.

pot o' gold
Prepare the basic cupcake recipe. Tint the frosting green. For each cupcake, frost the top, but omit basic decorations. Place a hollow chocolate cup in the center of the cupcake. Fill with small gold-covered chocolate coins or gold nuggets candies. Arch a piece of rainbow licorice or rope candy from one side of the cupcake to the other.

variations

how does your garden grow?

see base recipe page 260

strawberry fields forever
Prepare the basic cupcake recipe. Substitute small red candies or balls for candy vegetables.

magic bean garden
Prepare the basic cupcake recipe. Substitute small pastel jelly beans for candy vegetables.

diggin' in the dirt
Prepare the basic cupcake recipe. Omit the coconut and candy vegetables. Poke and enlarge 3 holes in the top of each cupcake and partially insert a gummy worm in each hole.

variations

bride doll

see base recipe page 262

princess doll
Prepare the basic cupcake recipe. Tint the frosting a pale pink and use pink and purple sugar pearls and flowers.

bridesmaid doll
Prepare the basic cupcake recipe. Tint the frosting a pale blue and use blue sugar pearls and flowers.

red carpet doll
Prepare the basic cupcake recipe. Tint the frosting a dark blue or purple, smooth it over the body, and sprinkle it with edible metallic glitter.

variations

ruffles & pearls

see base recipe page 265

raspberry ruffles & pearls
Prepare the basic cupcake recipe. Tint the frosting and moldable chocolate pale pink and flavor with raspberry flavoring. Sprinkle with pink sugar pearls.

lemon ruffles & pearls
Prepare the basic cupcake recipe. Tint the frosting and moldable chocolate pale yellow and flavor with lemon extract. Sprinkle with yellow sugar pearls.

mocha ruffles
Prepare the basic cupcake recipe. Instead of preparing Moldable White Chocolate, substitute semisweet chocolate for the white chocolate and add 1/2 cup (4 fl. oz.) additional light corn syrup. Flavor the chocolate with 2 teaspoons coffee extract. Dust ruffles with cinnamon sugar.

variations

morning latte

see base recipe page 266

hot chocolate
Prepare the basic cupcake recipe. Omit the coffee flavoring in the frosting.
Sprinkle chocolate sprinkles on top of each cupcake.

caramel macchiato
Prepare the basic cupcake recipe. Substitute prepared caramel ice cream
syrup for the coffee flavoring in the frosting. Drizzle prepared caramel ice
cream syrup on top of each cupcake.

chai
Substitute 1 1/2 recipes Chai Cupcakes (page 58) for basic Morning Latte
cupcakes. Dust top of each cupcake with a mixture of 1 tablespoon raw
sugar combined with 1 teaspoon each: ground cardamom, nutmeg, cloves,
and cinnamon.

variations

aquarium

see base recipe page 268

sea volcano
Tint half the frosting sea blue, the other half orange-red. Omit the candy fish. For each cupcake: Frost the top with blue. Use a knife to make "waves" around the perimeter of the cupcake. Carefully trim the pointed end off a waffle sugar ice cream cone and place in the center of the cupcake to make a volcano. Spoon or pipe orange-red frosting to look like lava coming out of the volcano and down its side, to the sea below. Sprinkle the "lava" with candy rocks or crushed nut cookies.

gold miner's dream
Tint the frosting sea blue. Omit the candy fish. For each cupcake: Frost the top thickly with blue. Use a knife to make a 1 1/2-inch-wide, meandering stream channel down the middle of the cupcake. Spoon yellow or gold decorating sugar and candy rocks or crushed nut cookies in the channel.

bridge over troubled waters
Tint the frosting sea blue. Omit the candy fish. For each cupcake: Frost the top thickly with blue. Use a knife to make "waves" around the perimeter of the cupcake. Lay a stick of fruit-striped candy across the center of the cupcake. Curve a pipe cleaner or chenille stick in coordinating colors to arch over on either side of the candy to form a suspension bridge.

variations

garden hat

see base recipe page 270

sombrero
Prepare the basic cupcake recipe. Omit the decorations. For each cupcake, frost the top. Place a large yellow gumdrop in the center. Arrange miniature or small pieces of gumdrops in assorted colors around perimeter of the cupcake.

santa hat
Prepare the basic cupcake recipe. Omit the decorations. Leave half the frosting white, the other half red. For each cupcake, frost the top with white. Carefully trim the pointed end off a waffle sugar ice cream cone and place the cone in the center of the cupcake to make a Santa hat. Pipe red frosting to cover the cone. Top with a large marshmallow.

red hat
Prepare the basic cupcake recipe. Omit gum. Tint the frosting red. For each cupcake, frost the top. Sandwich two vanilla wafers together with frosting and place in the center of the cupcake. Frost over that. Press a 7-inch stick of twisted black licorice to form a band around the stacked wafers, crossing the ends. Decorate around the hat band with red candy balls and flowers.

index